HEAVY HORSE COLORING BOOK

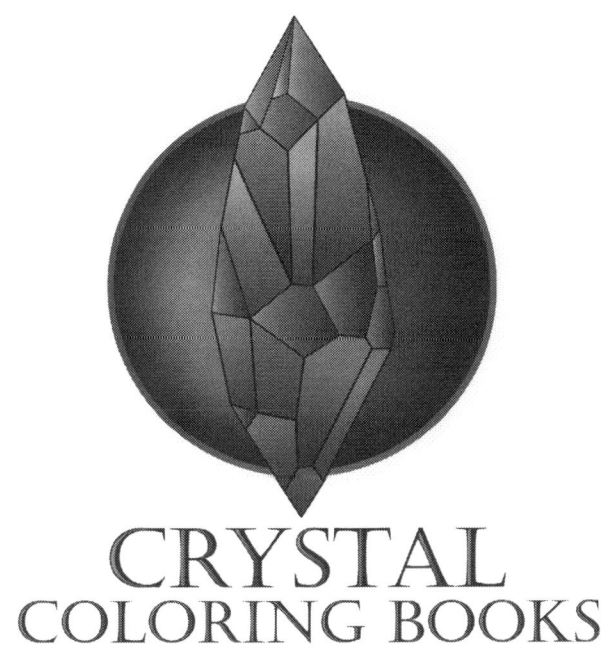

CRYSTAL COLORING BOOKS

Copyright © 2018 Crystal Coloring Books
All rights reserved.

ISBN: 9781726668637

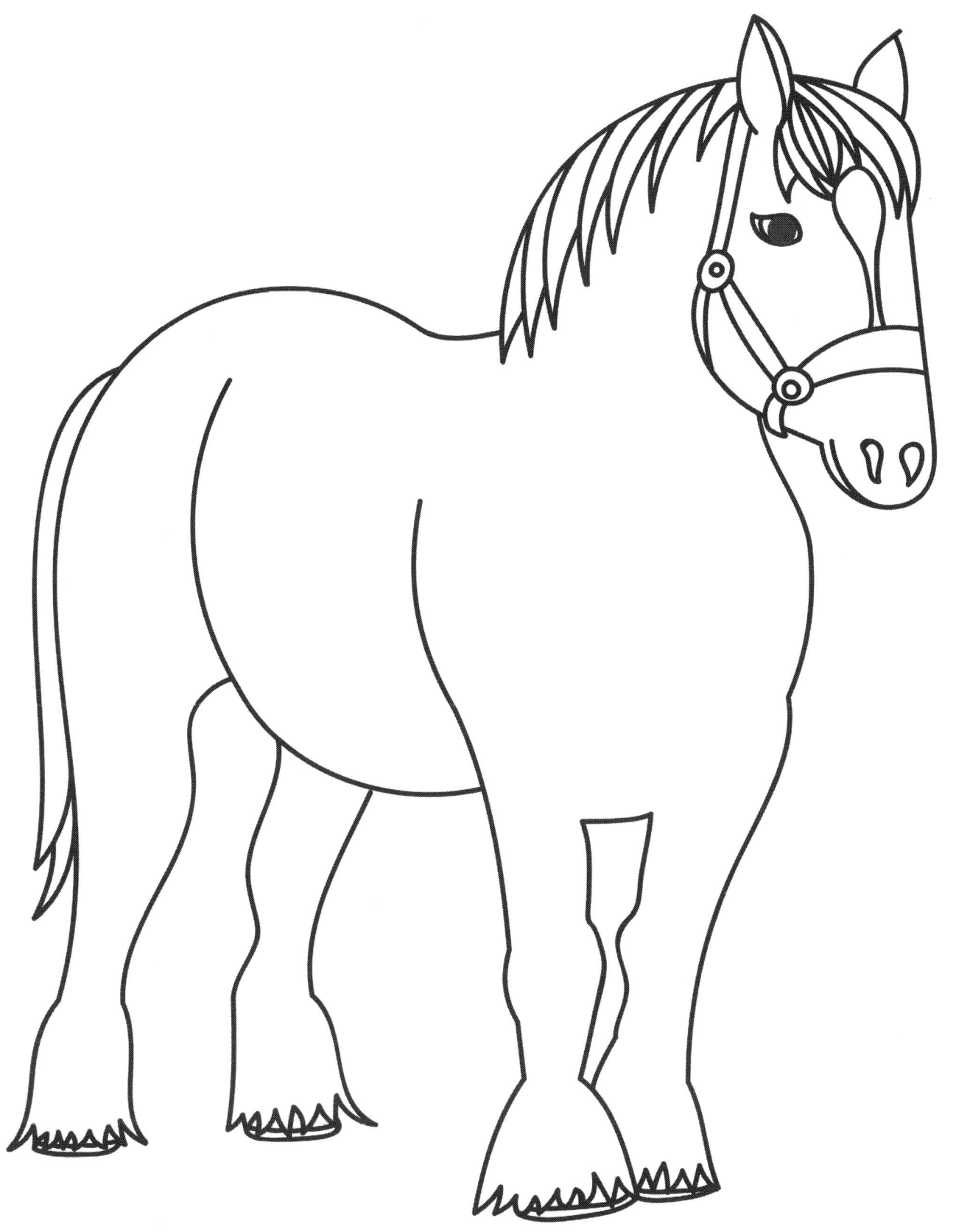

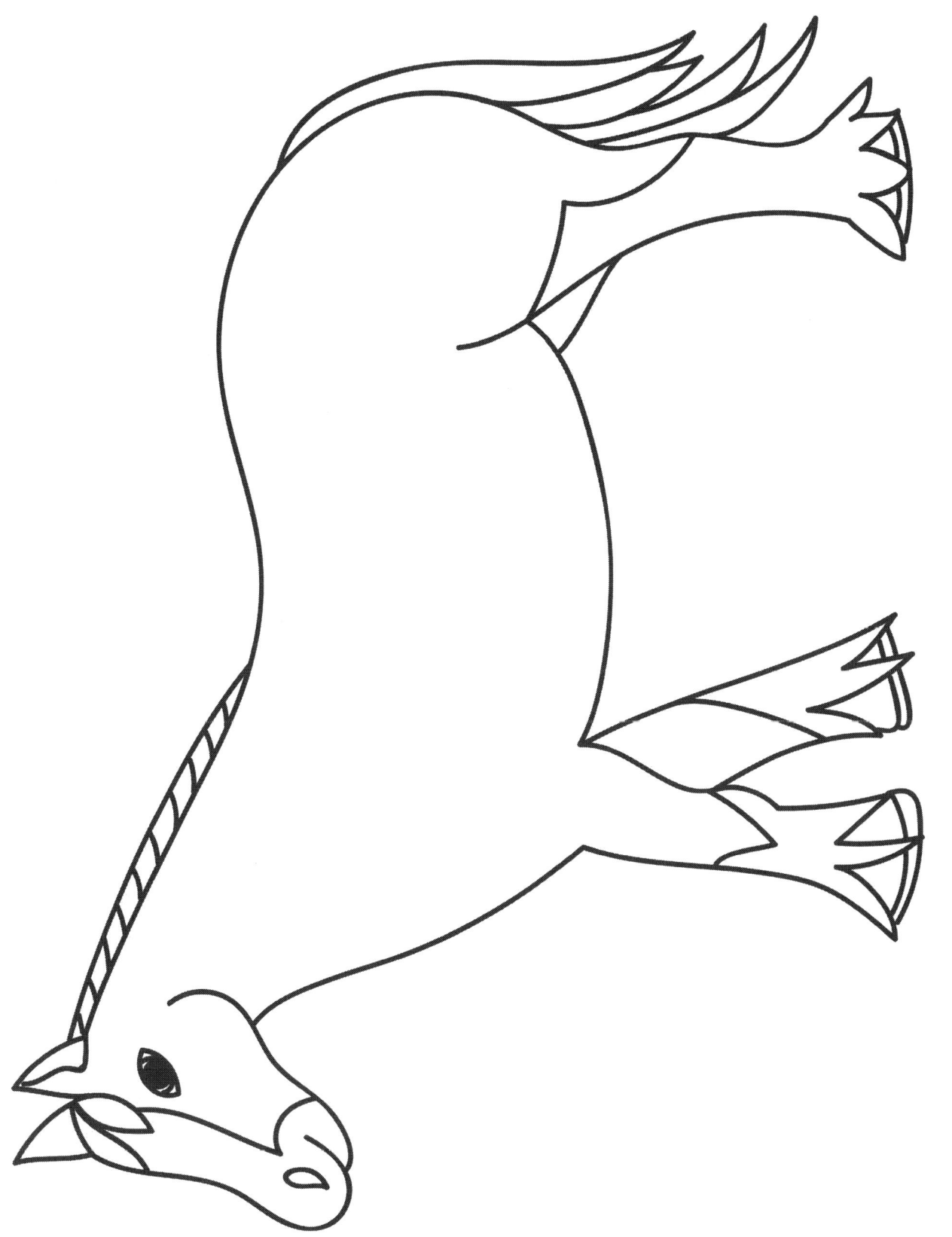

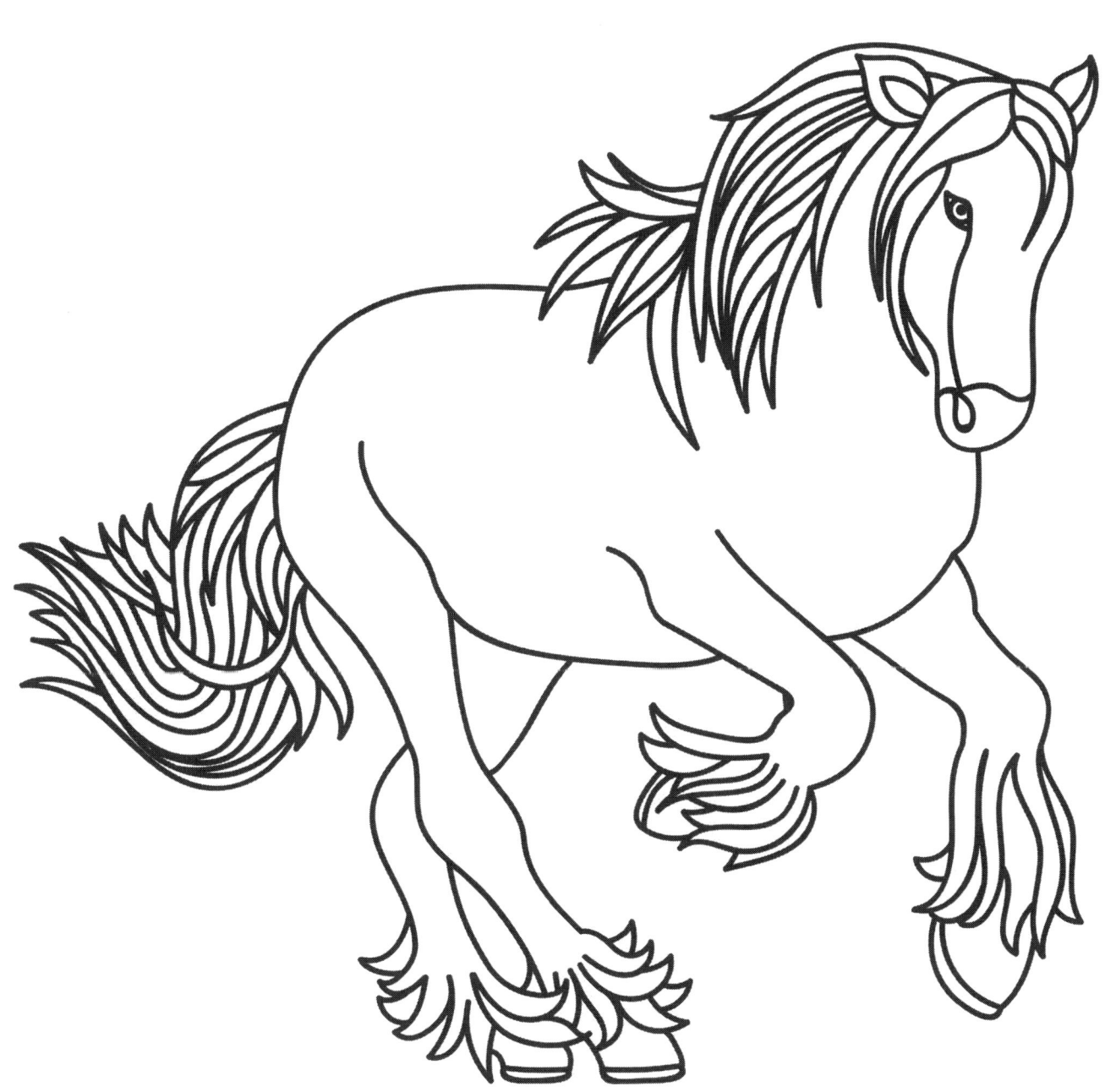

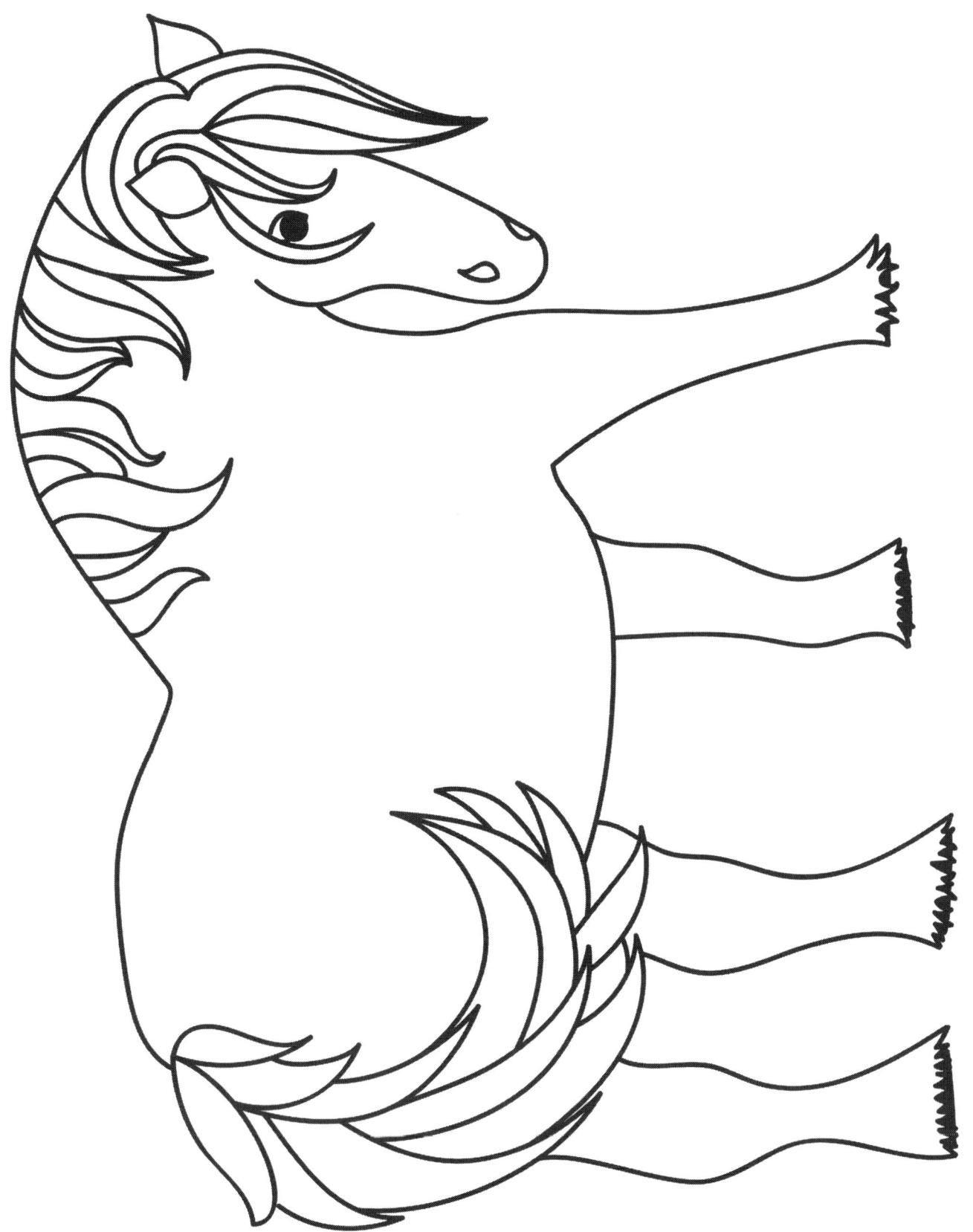

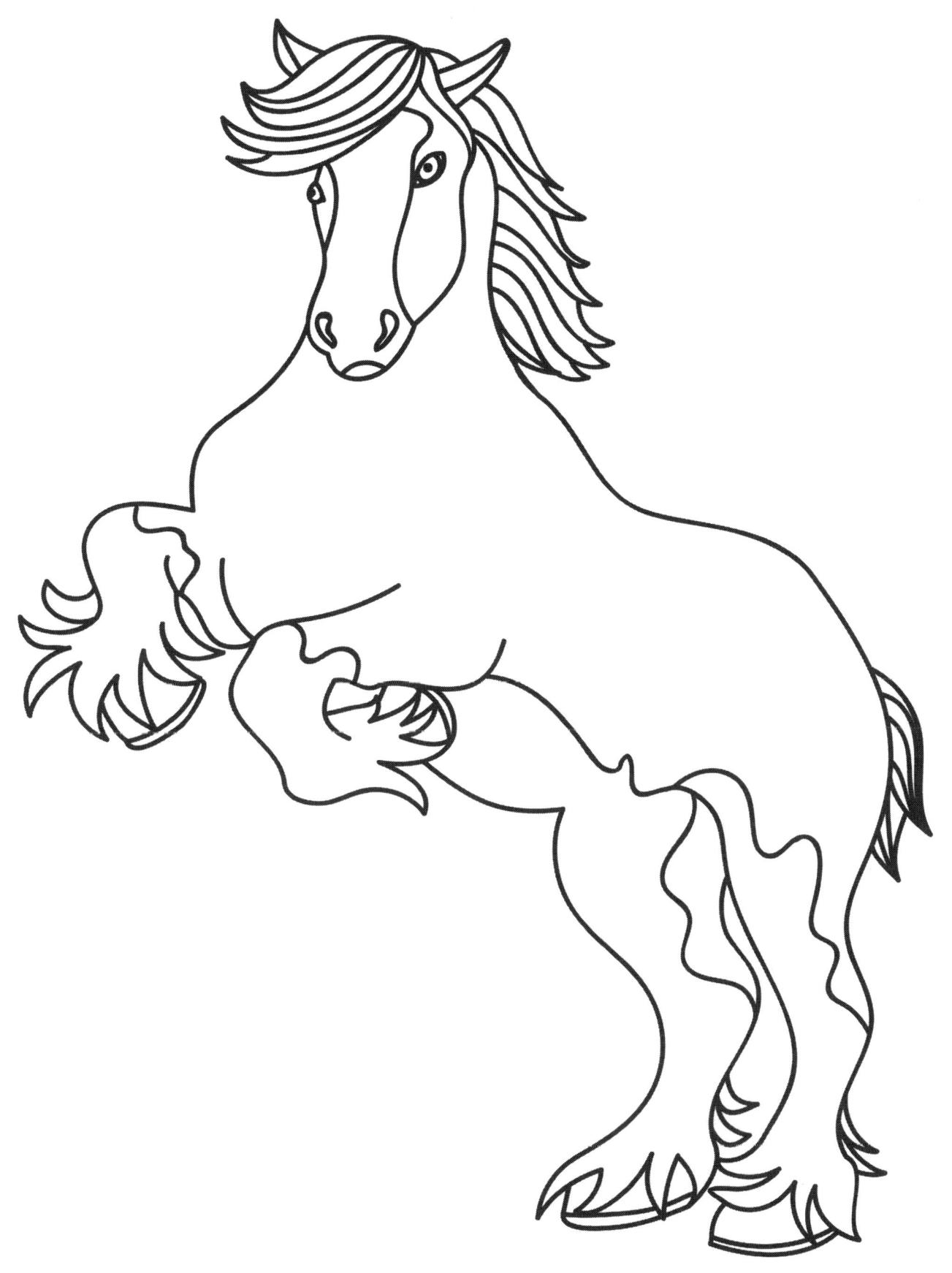

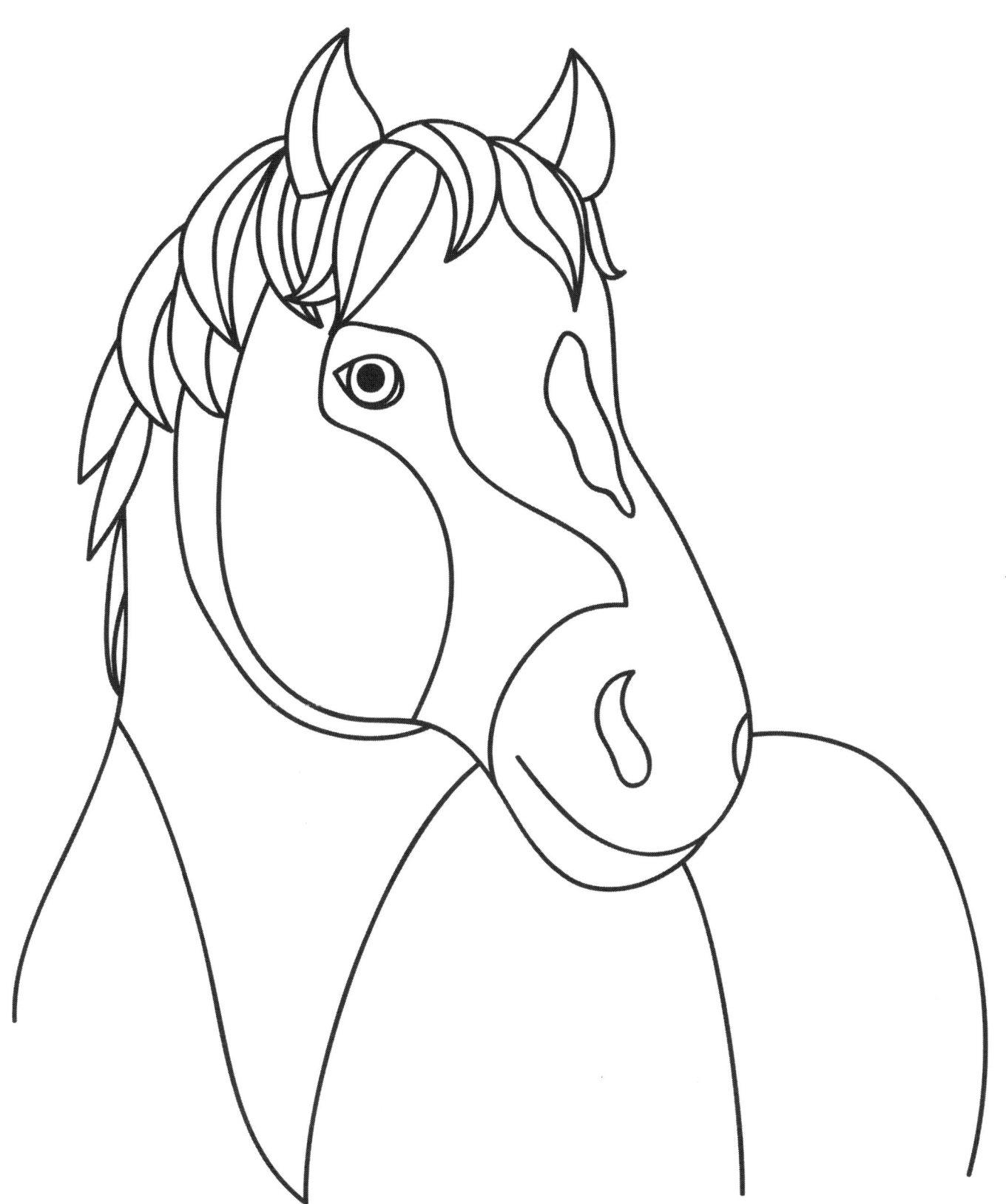

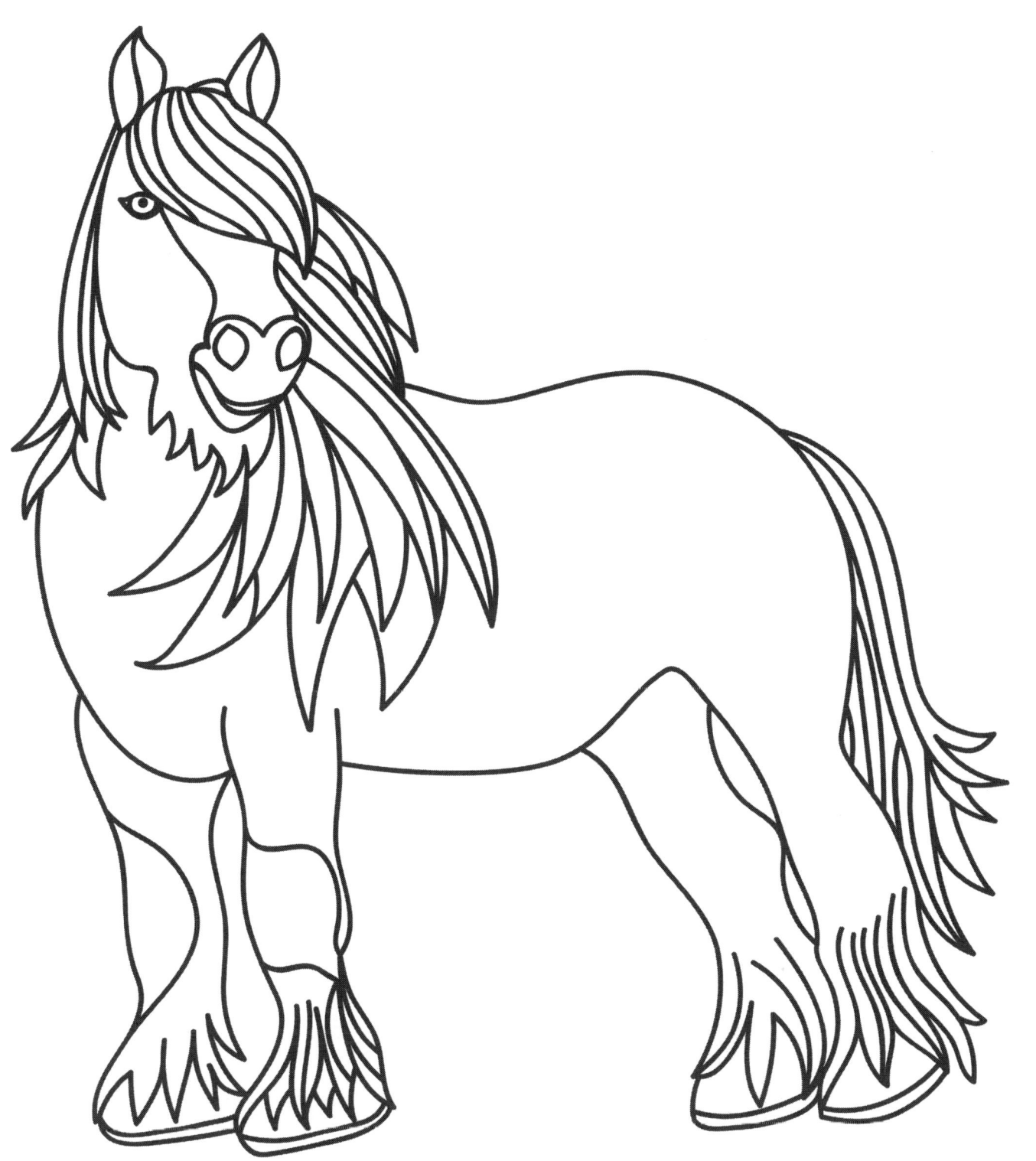

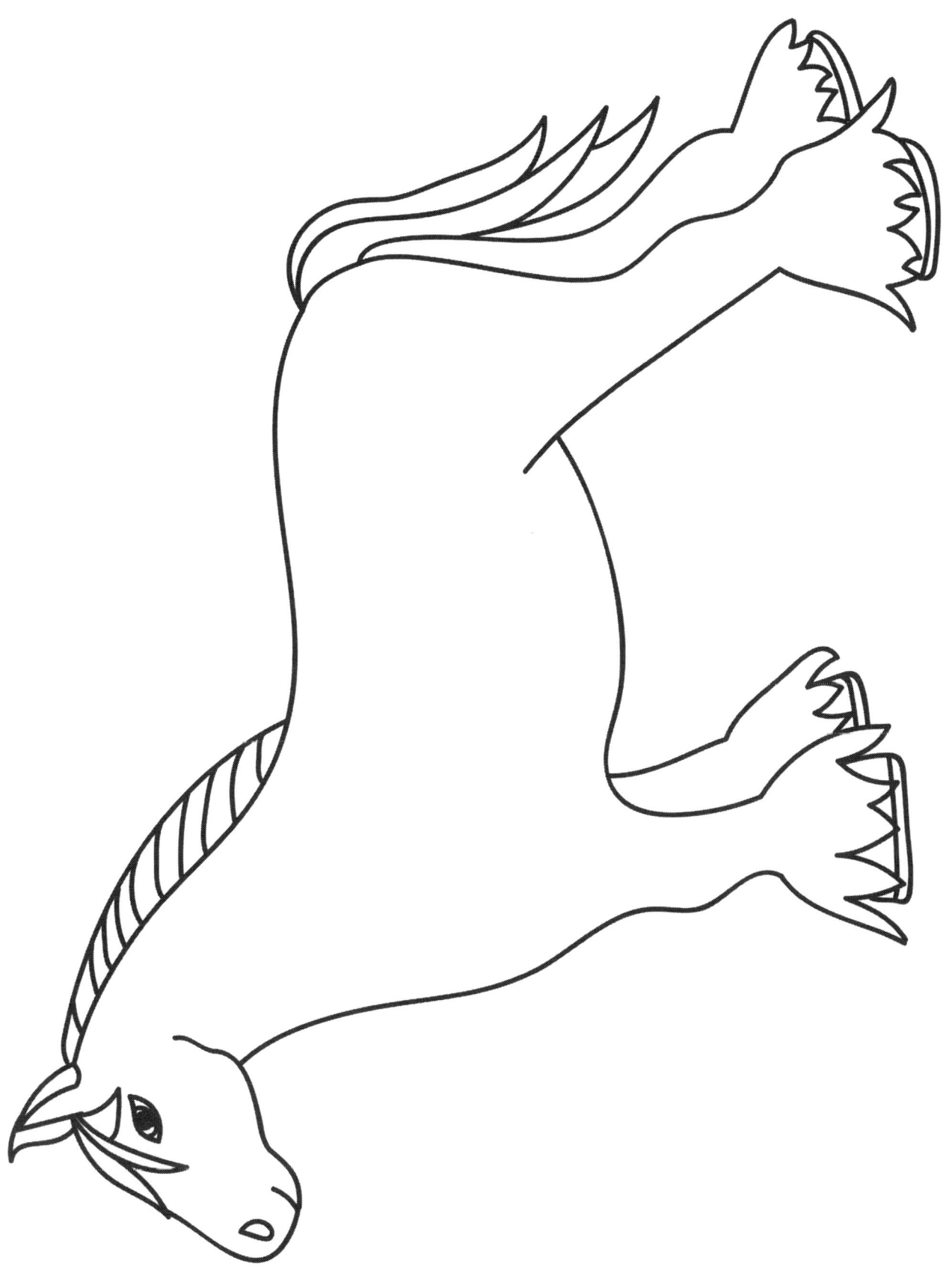

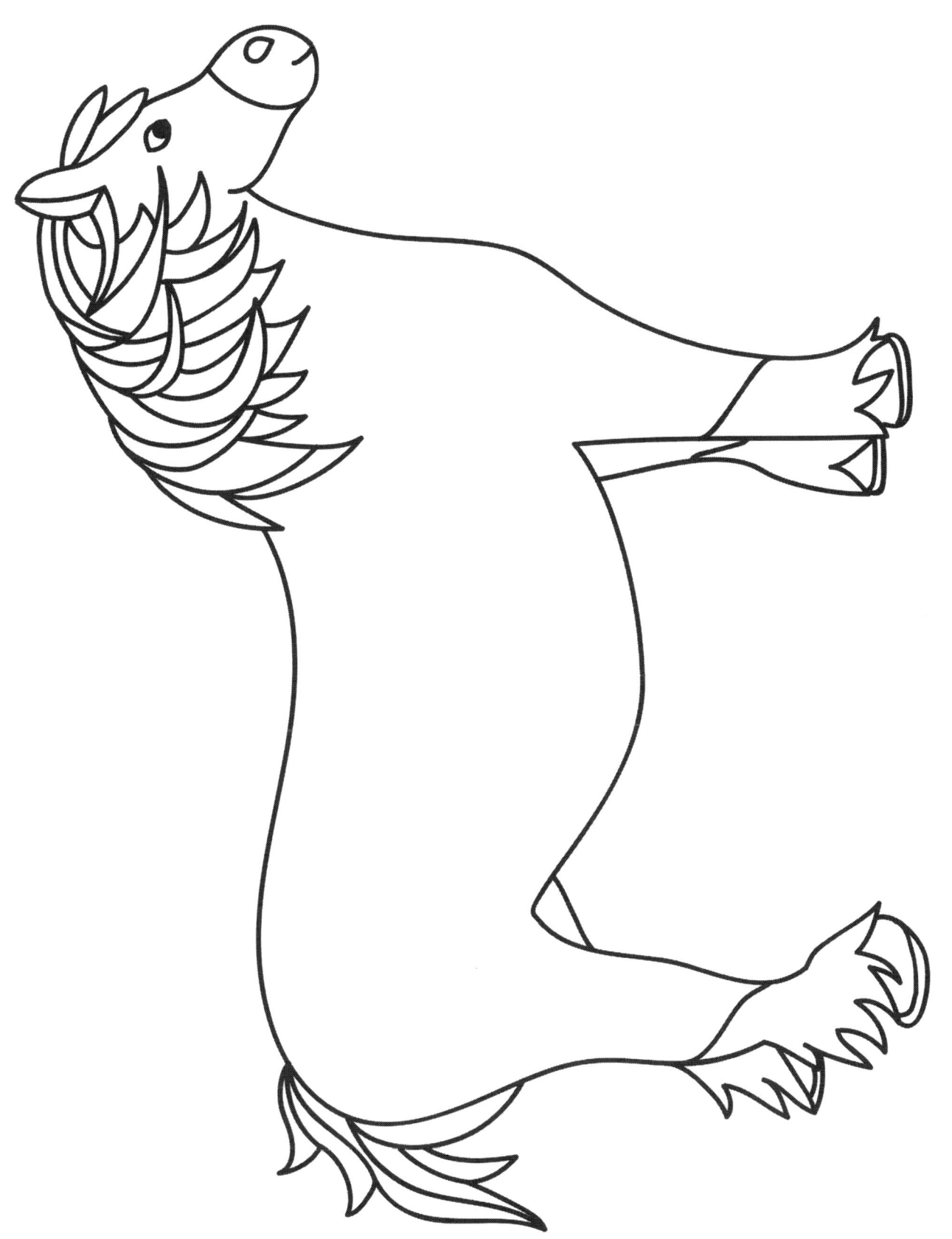

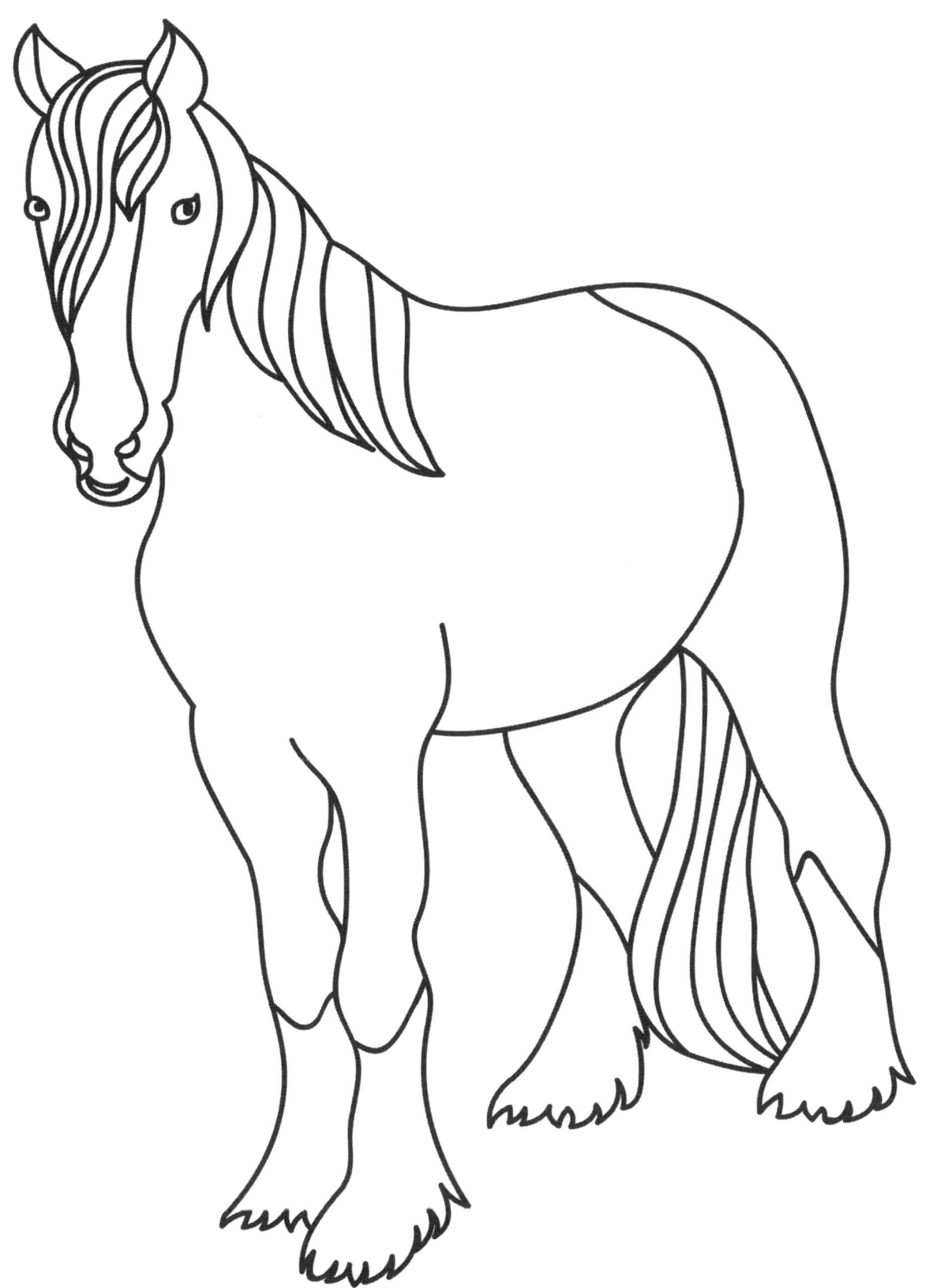

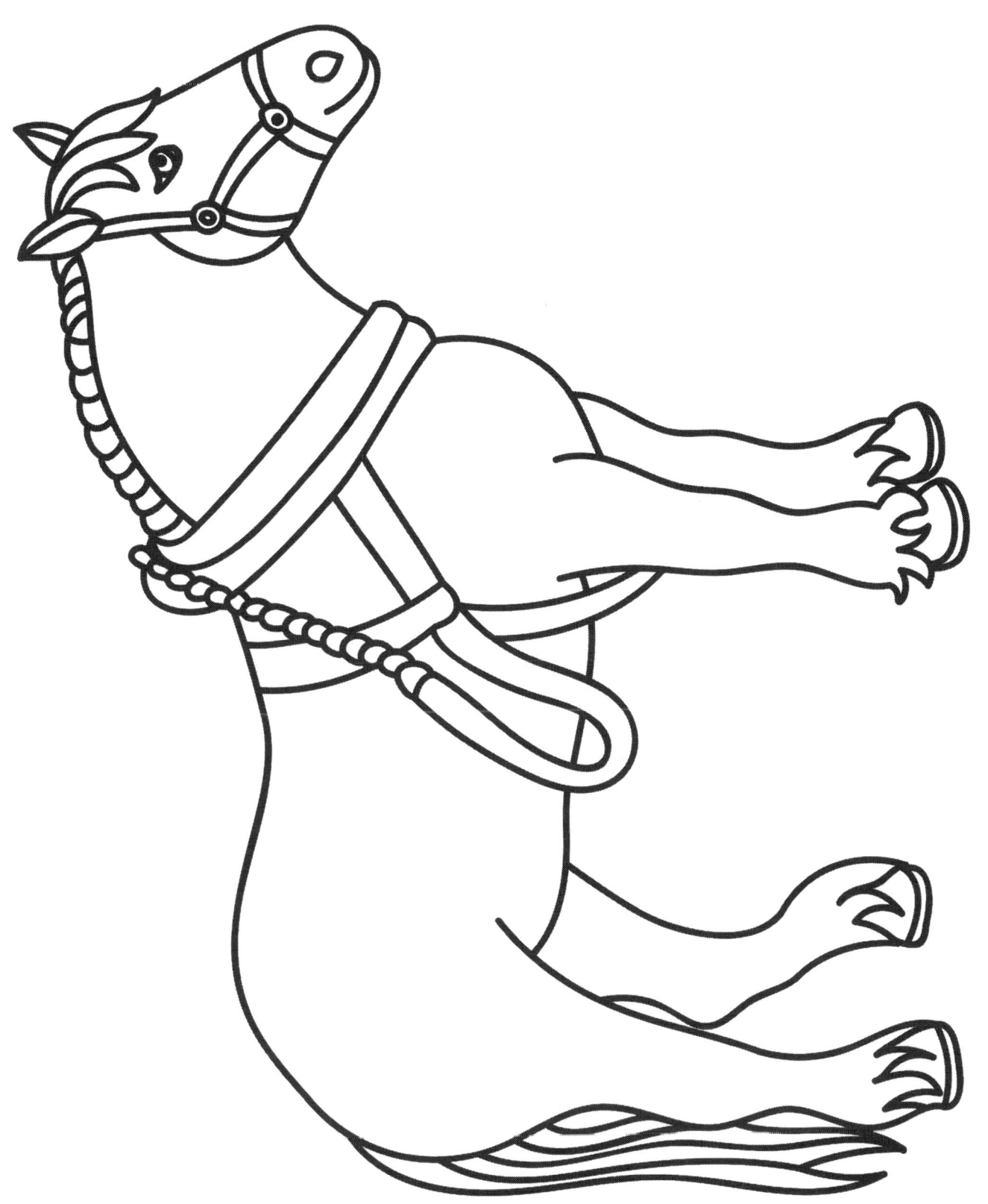

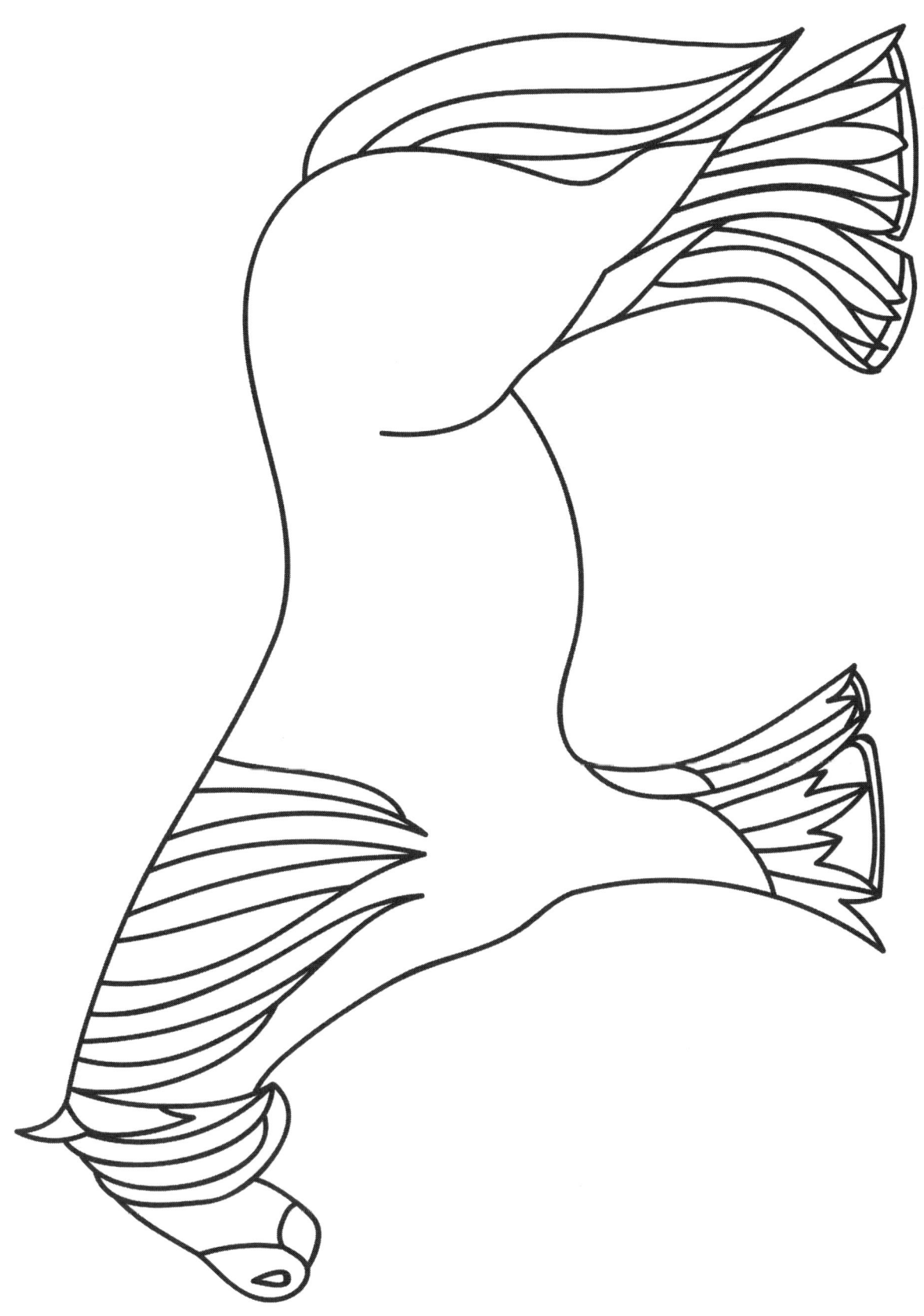

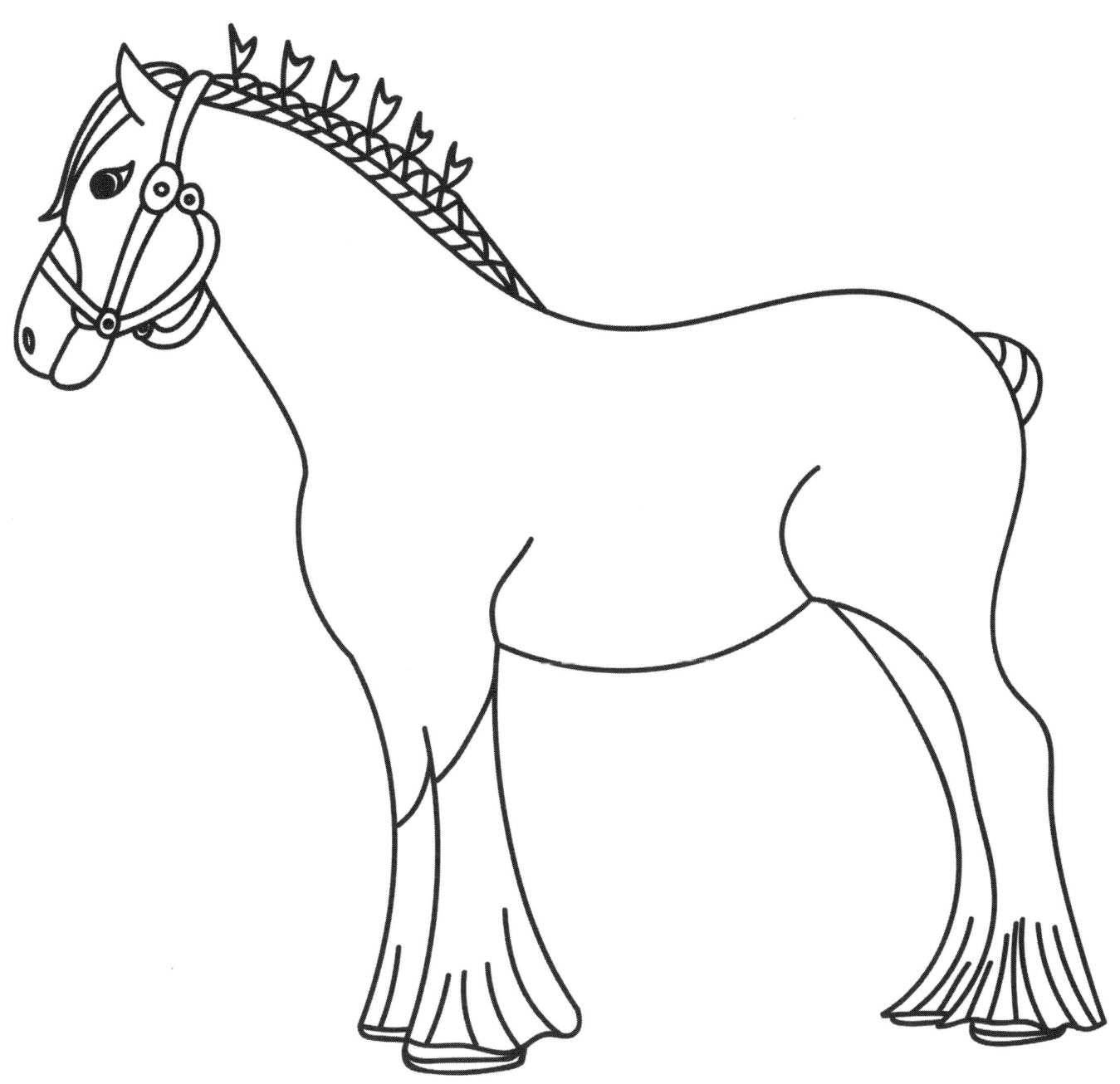

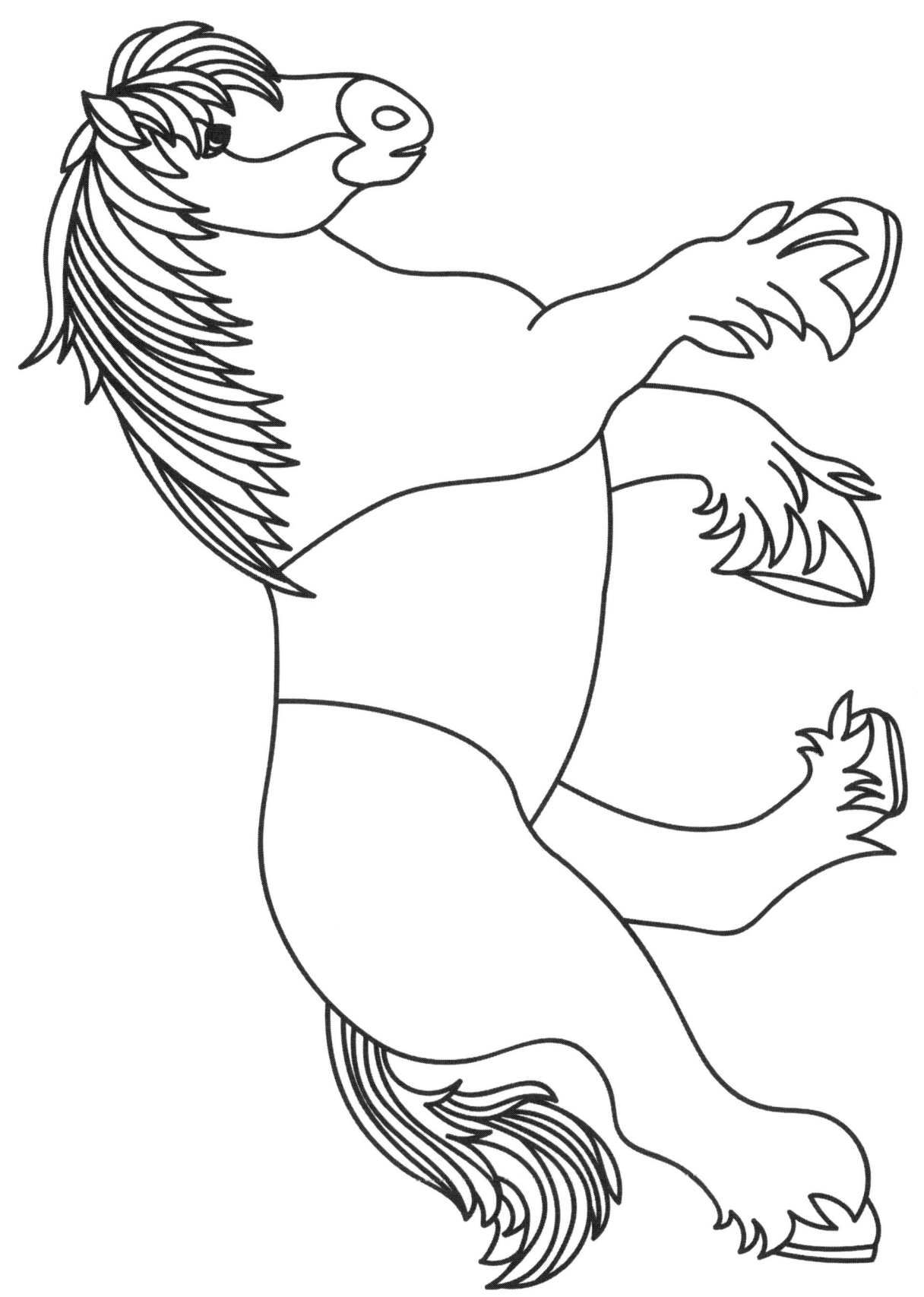

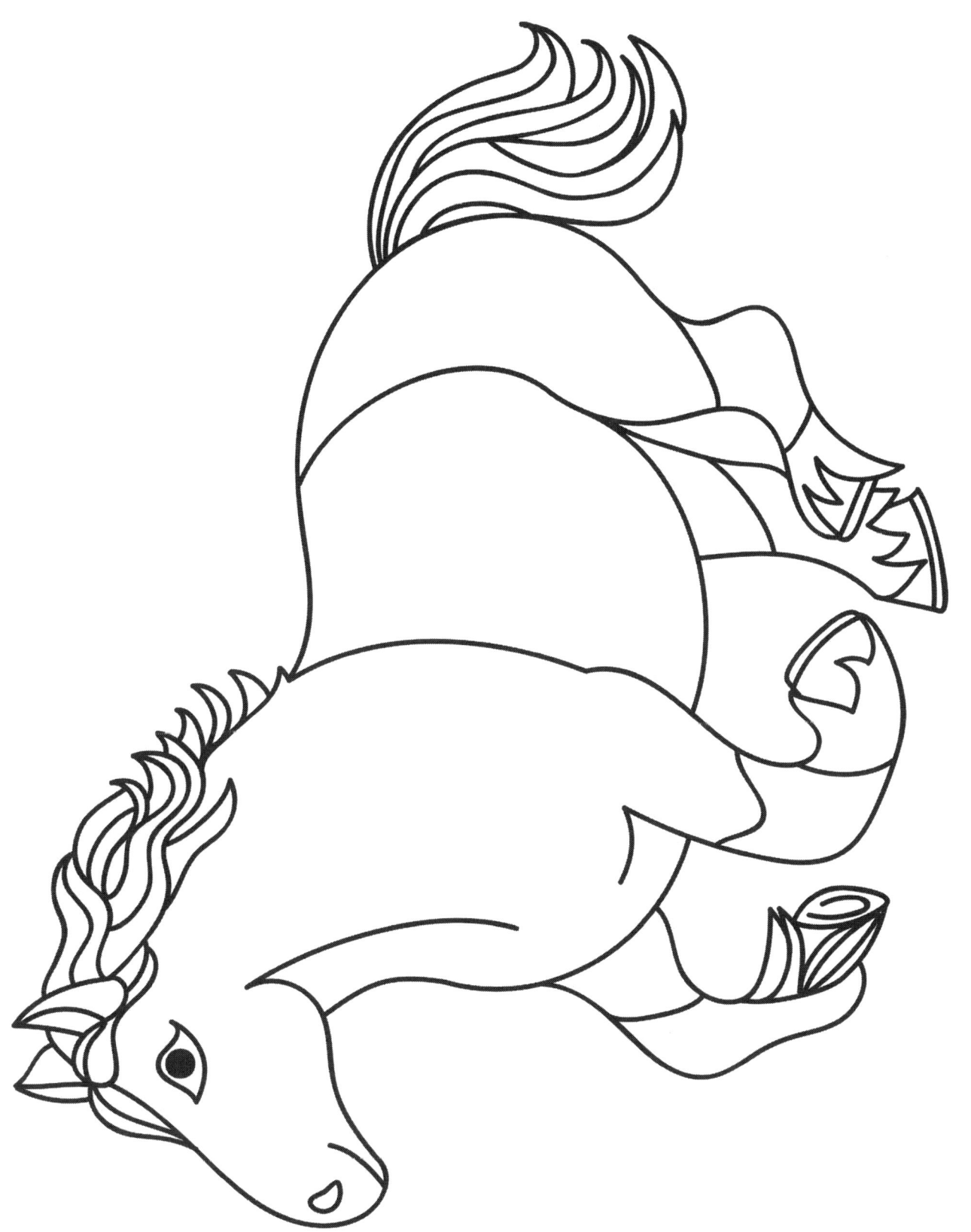

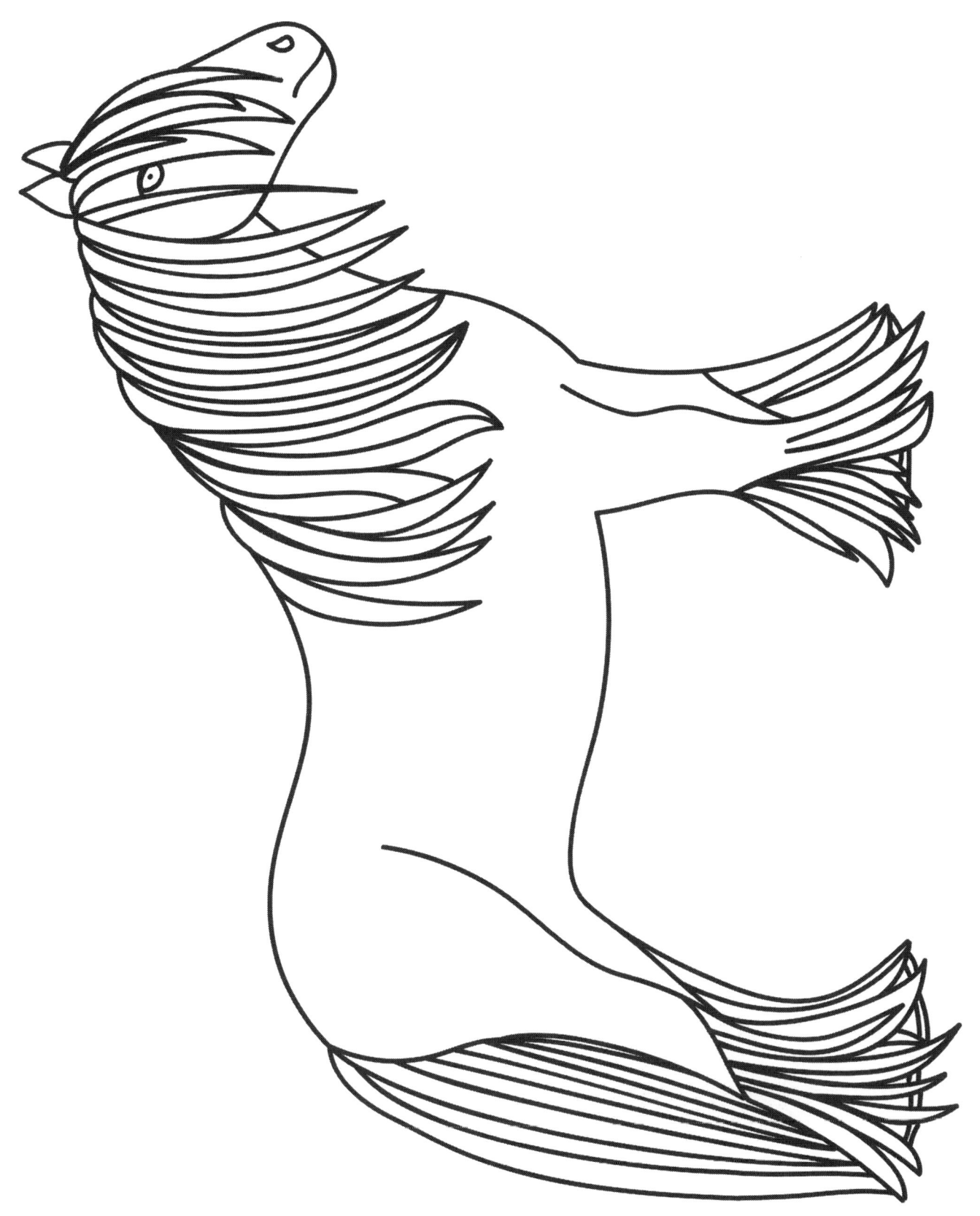

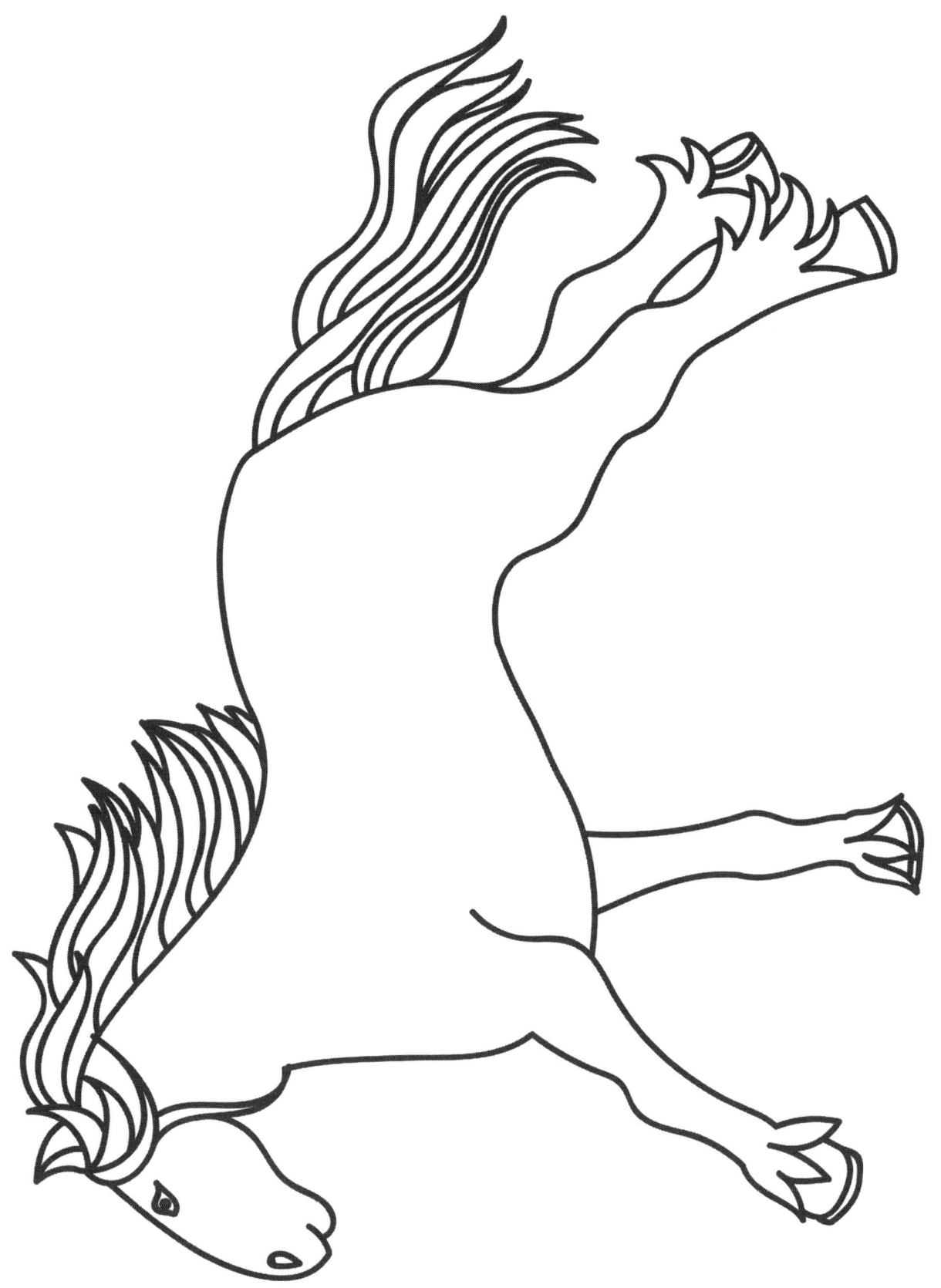

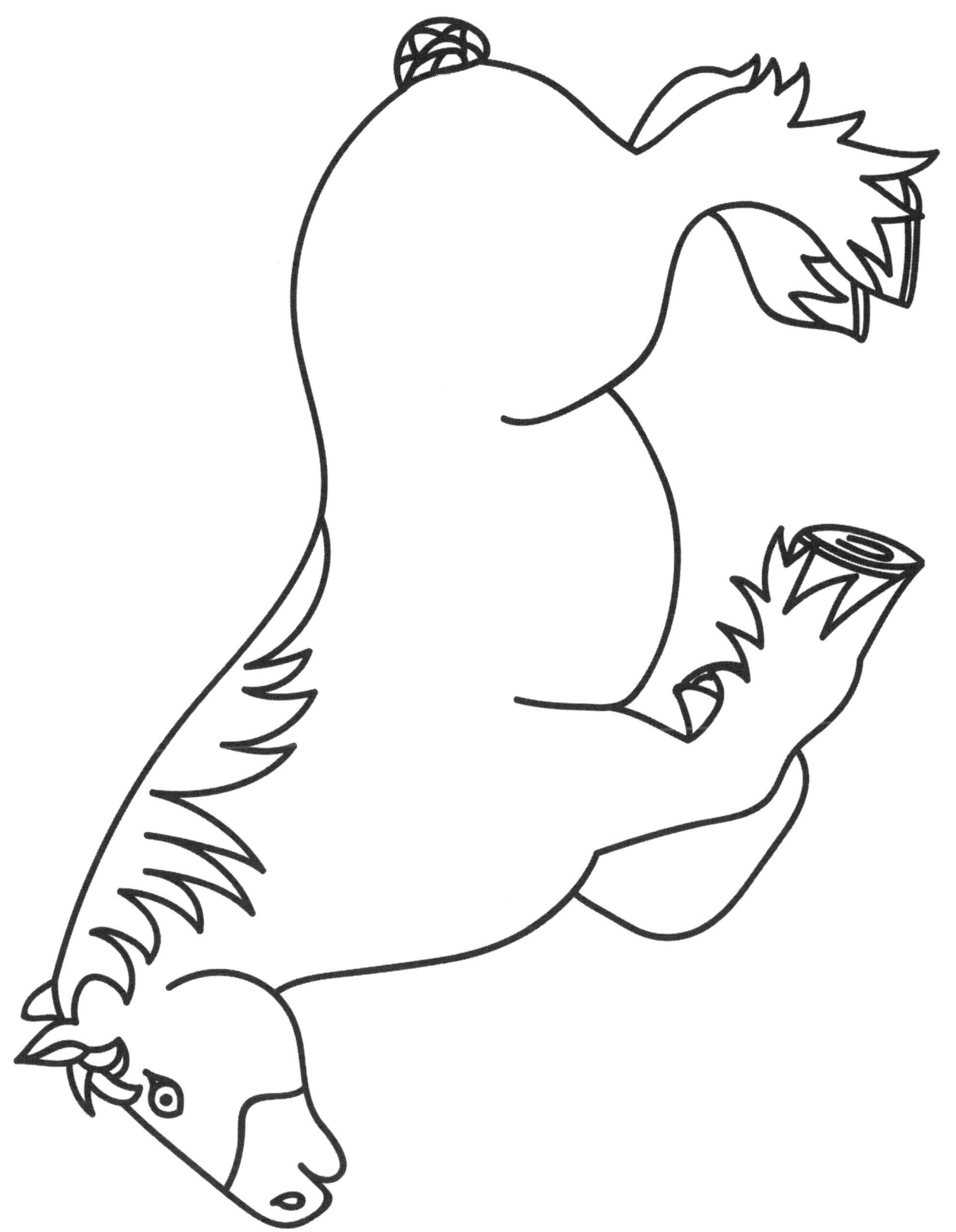

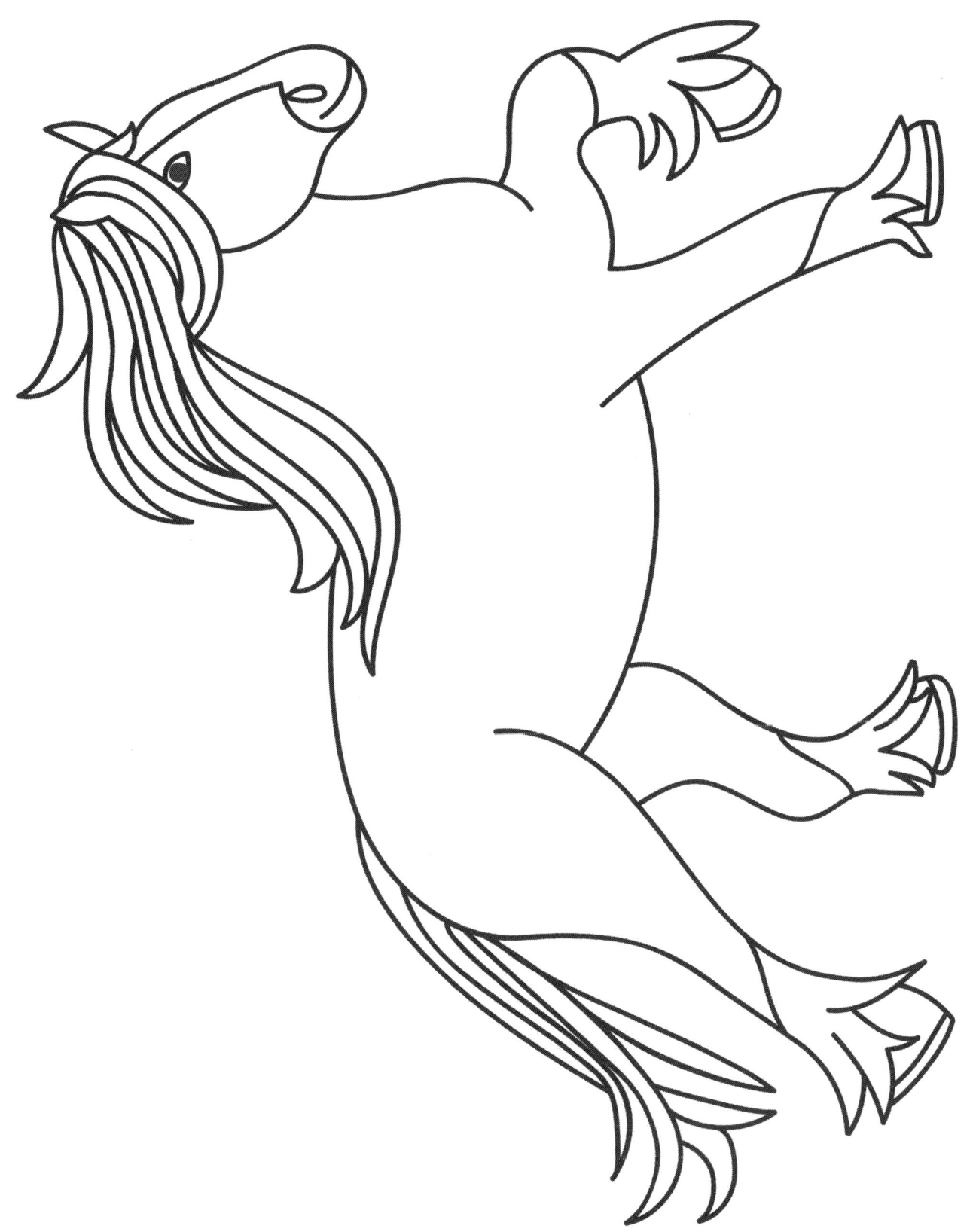

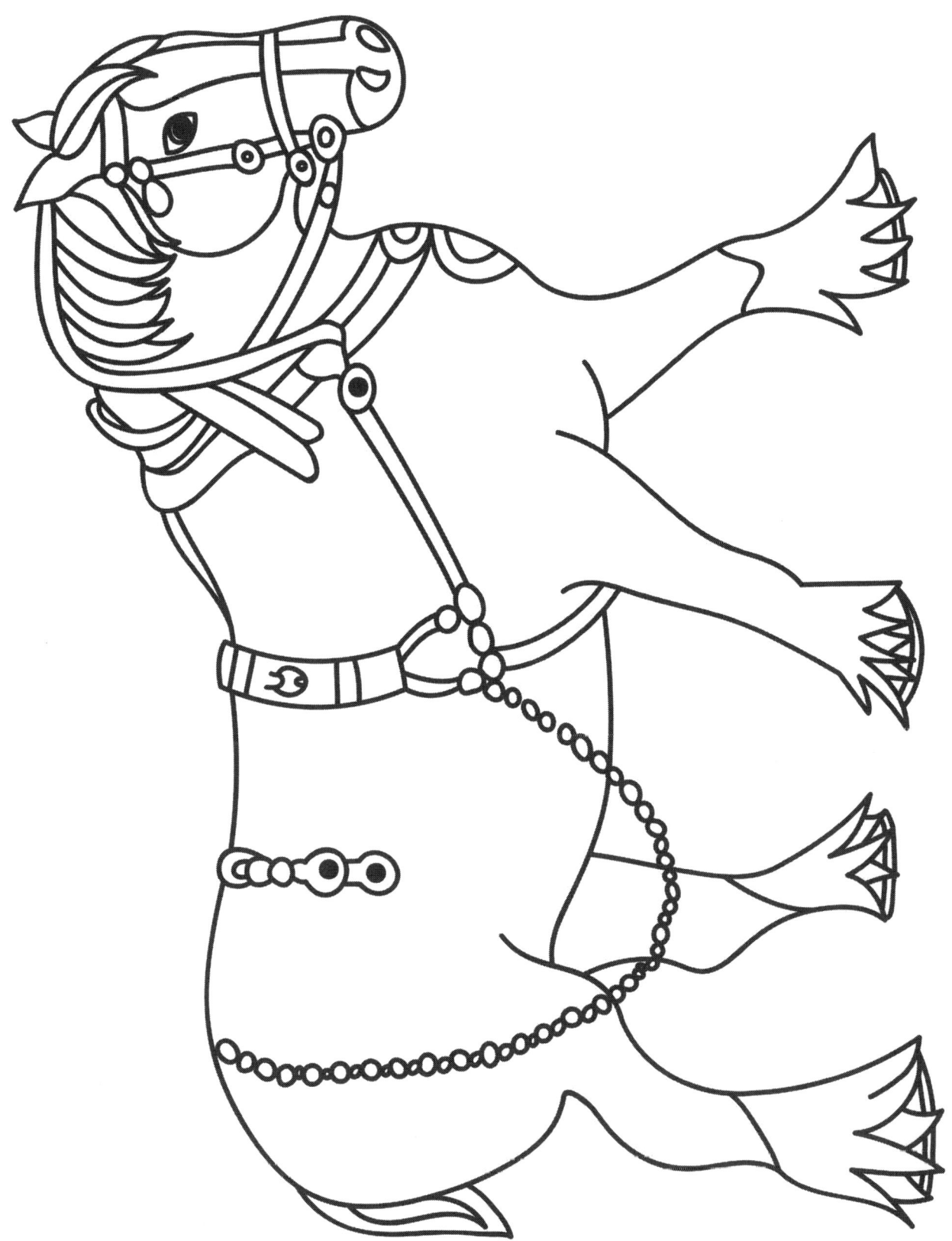

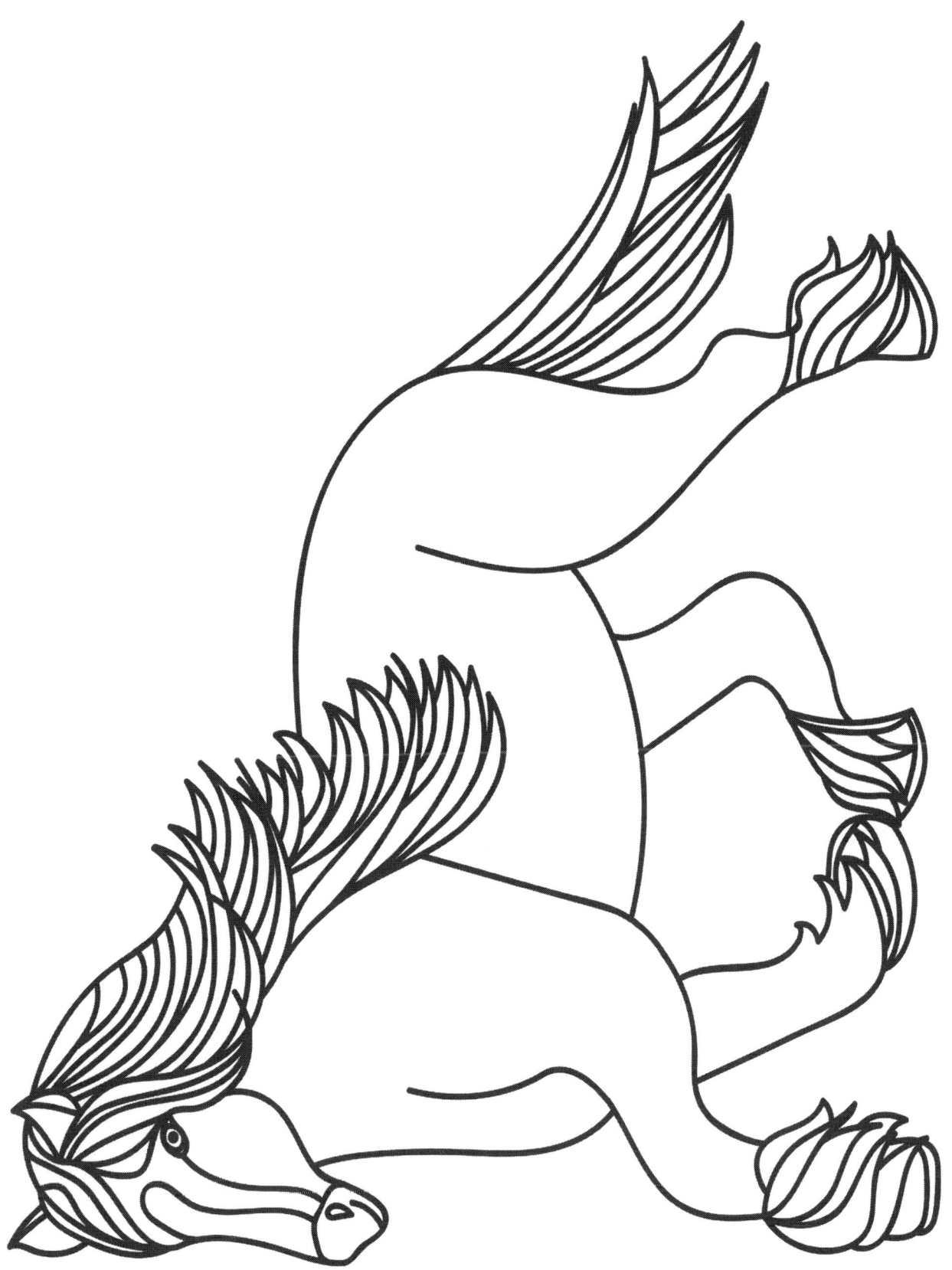

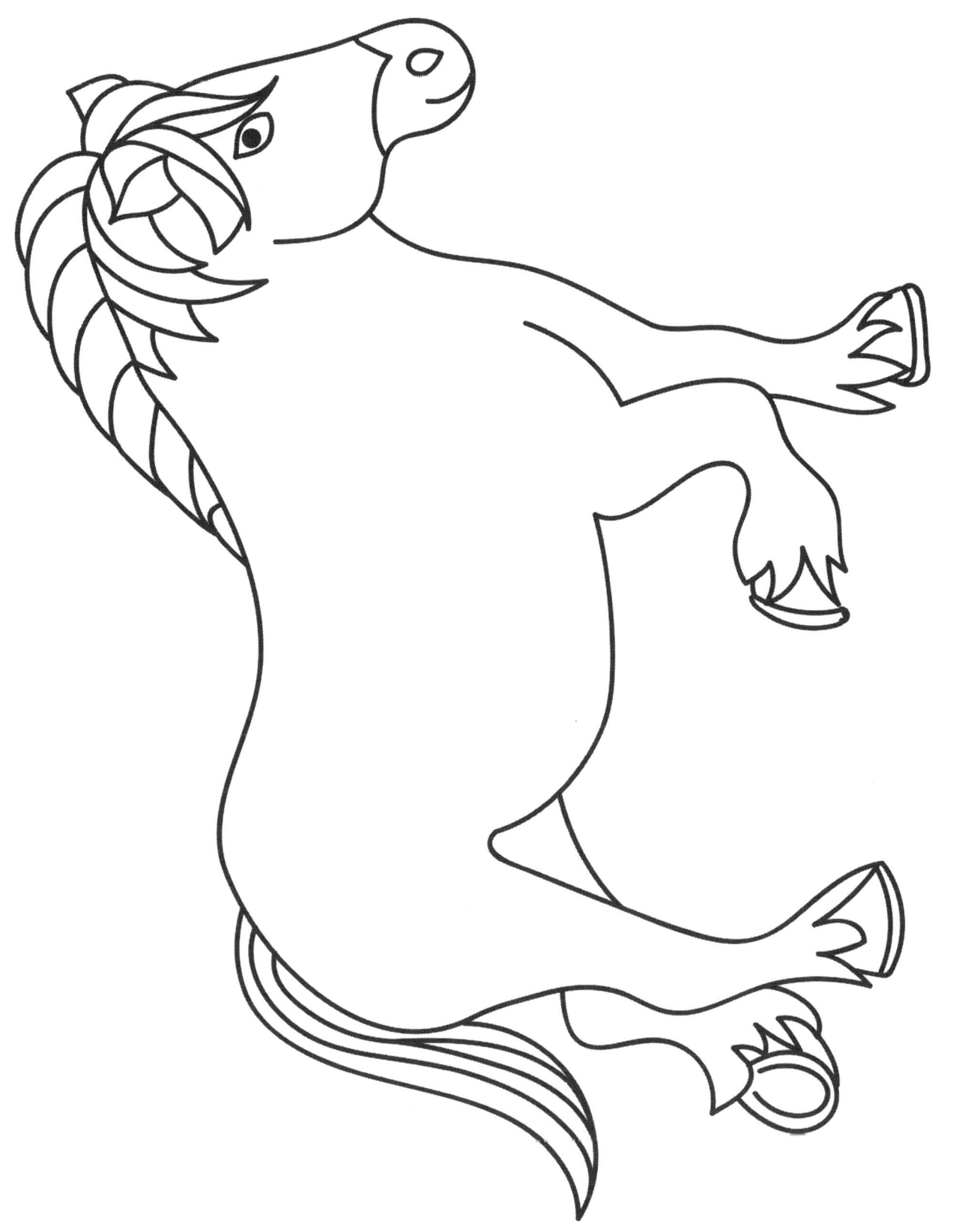

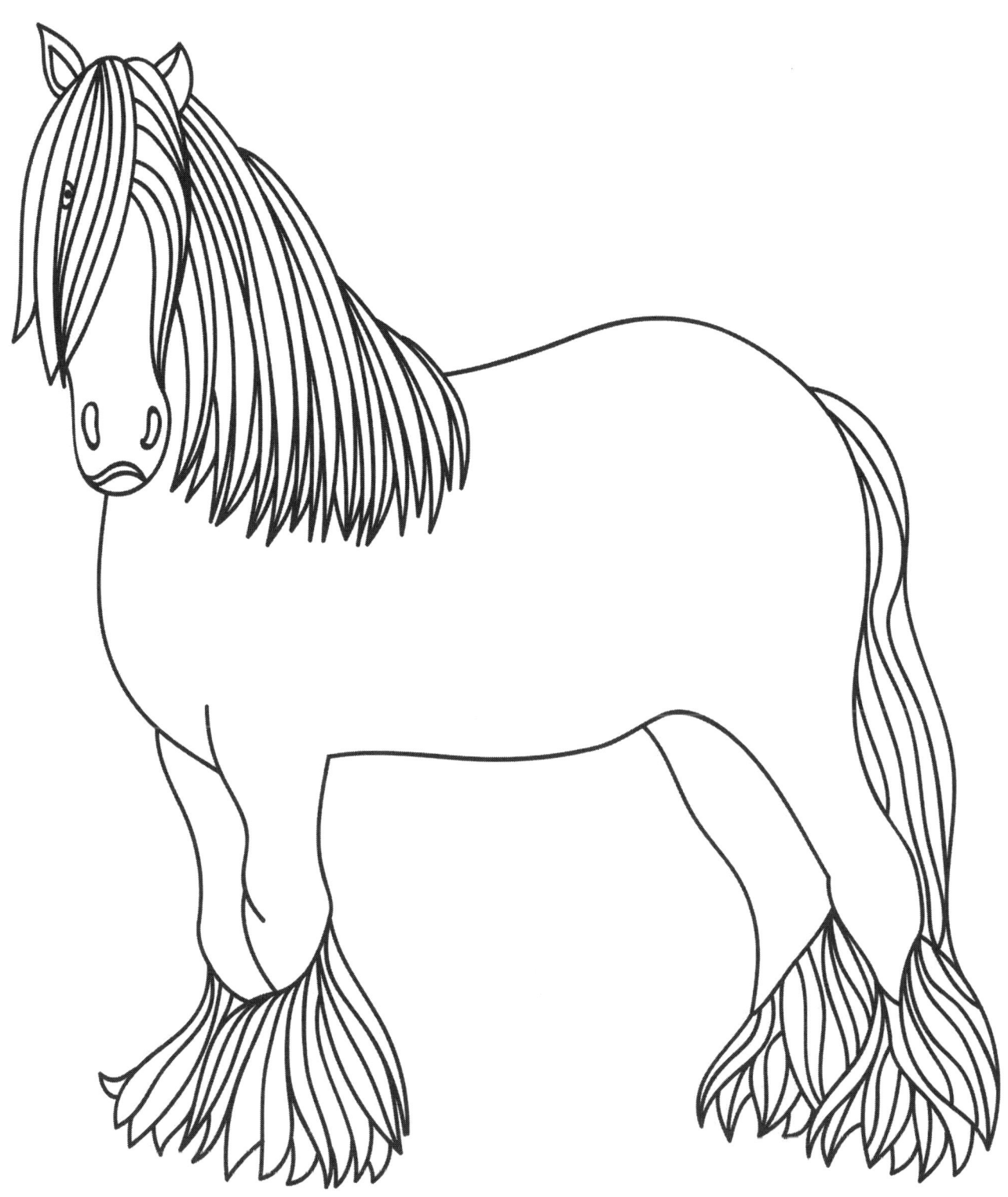

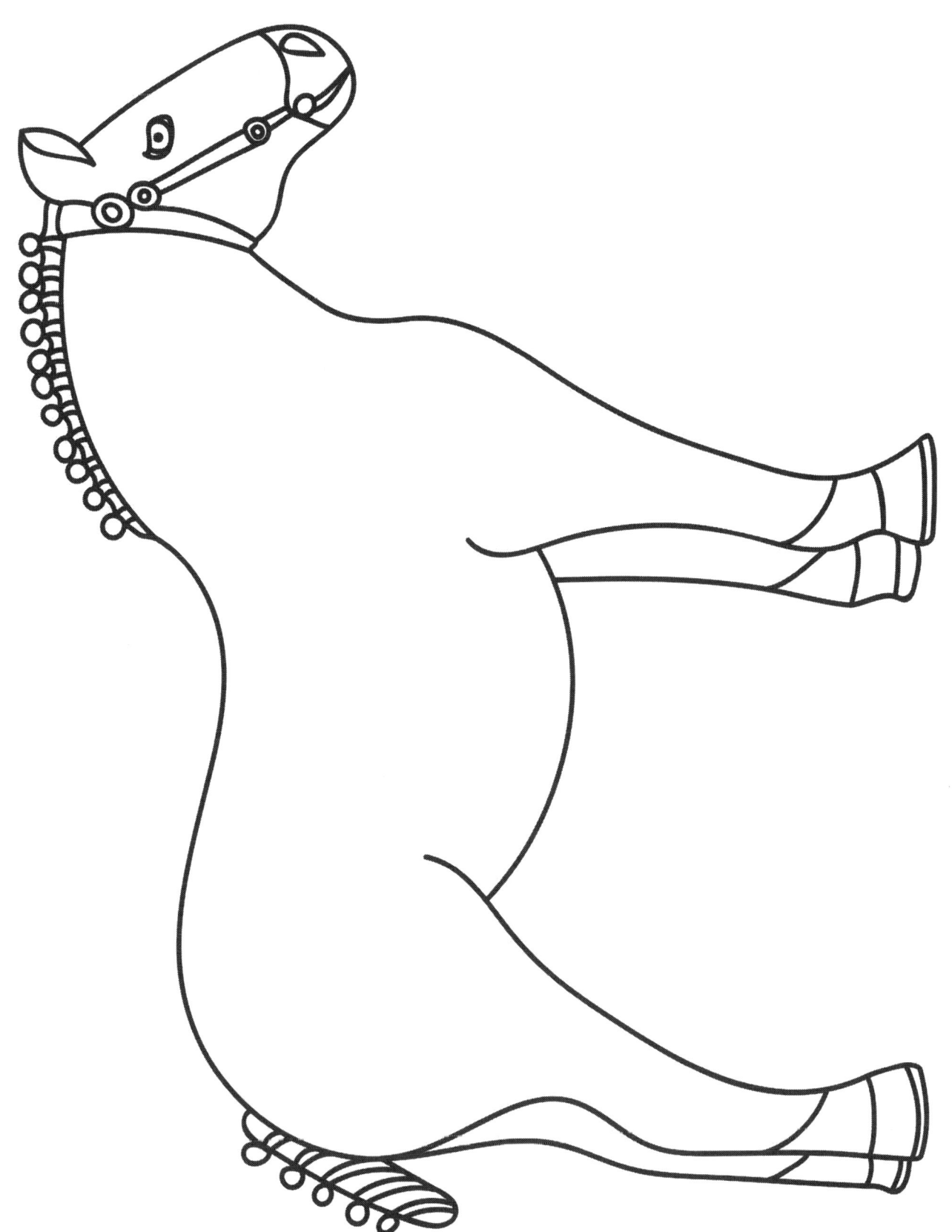

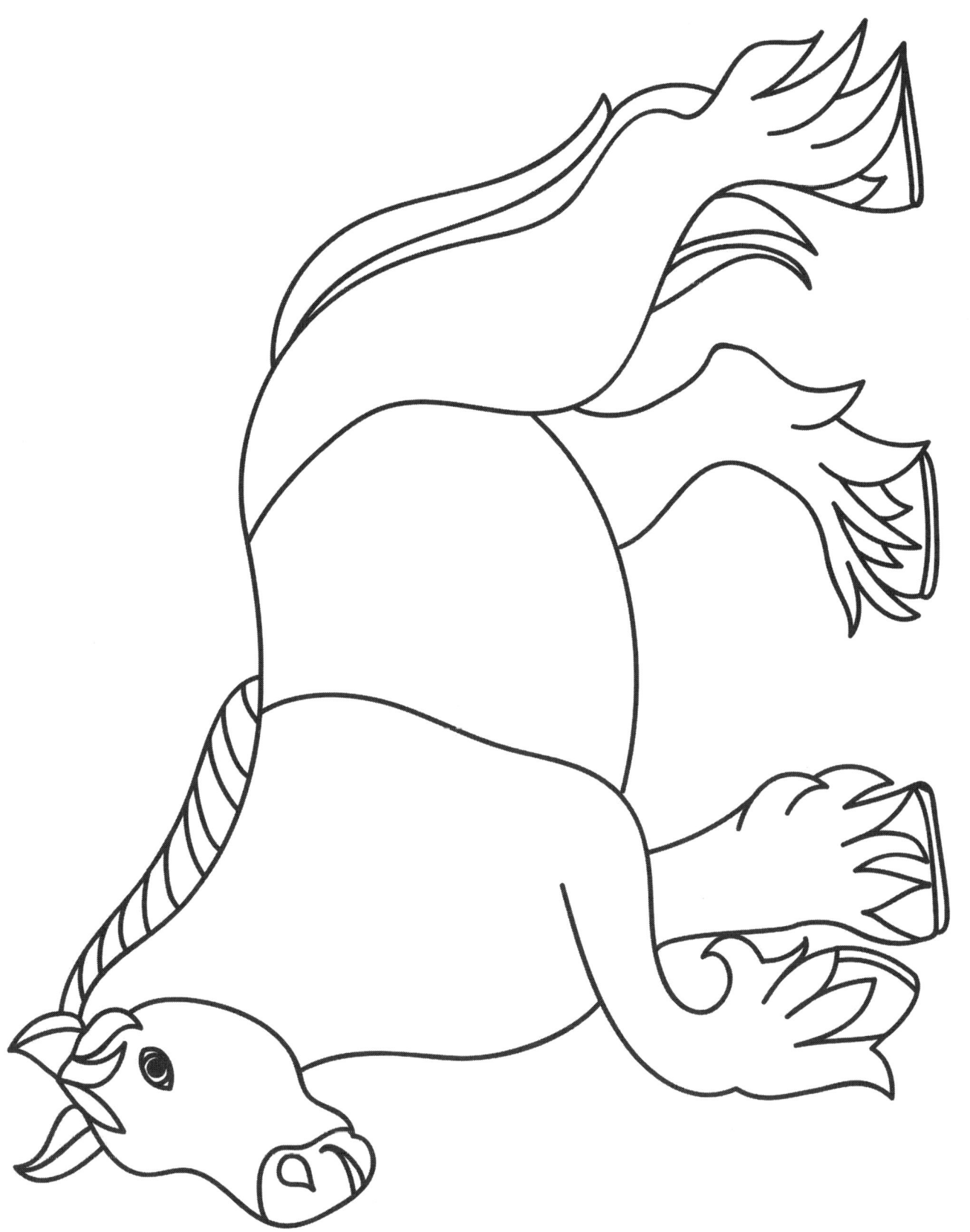

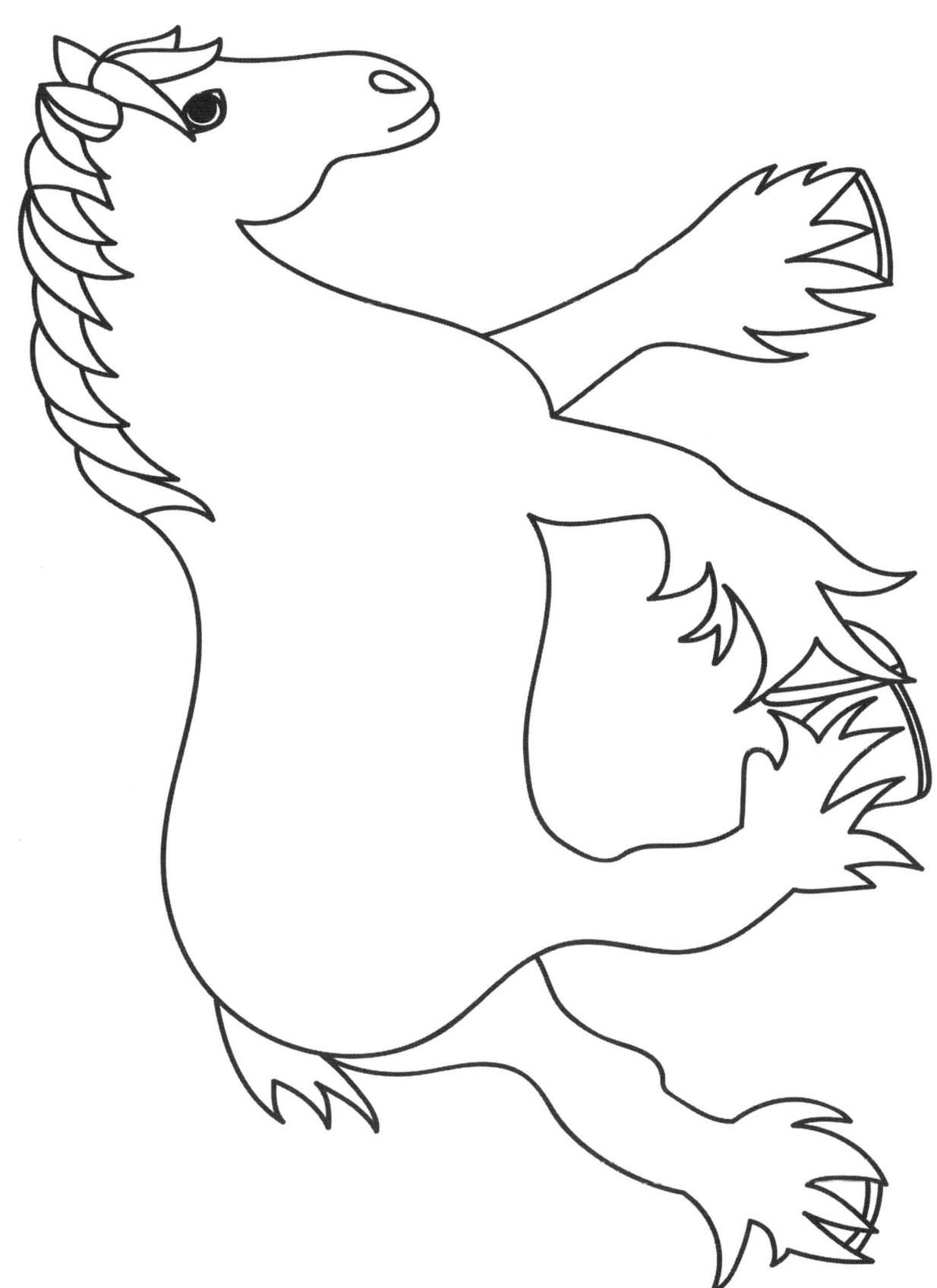

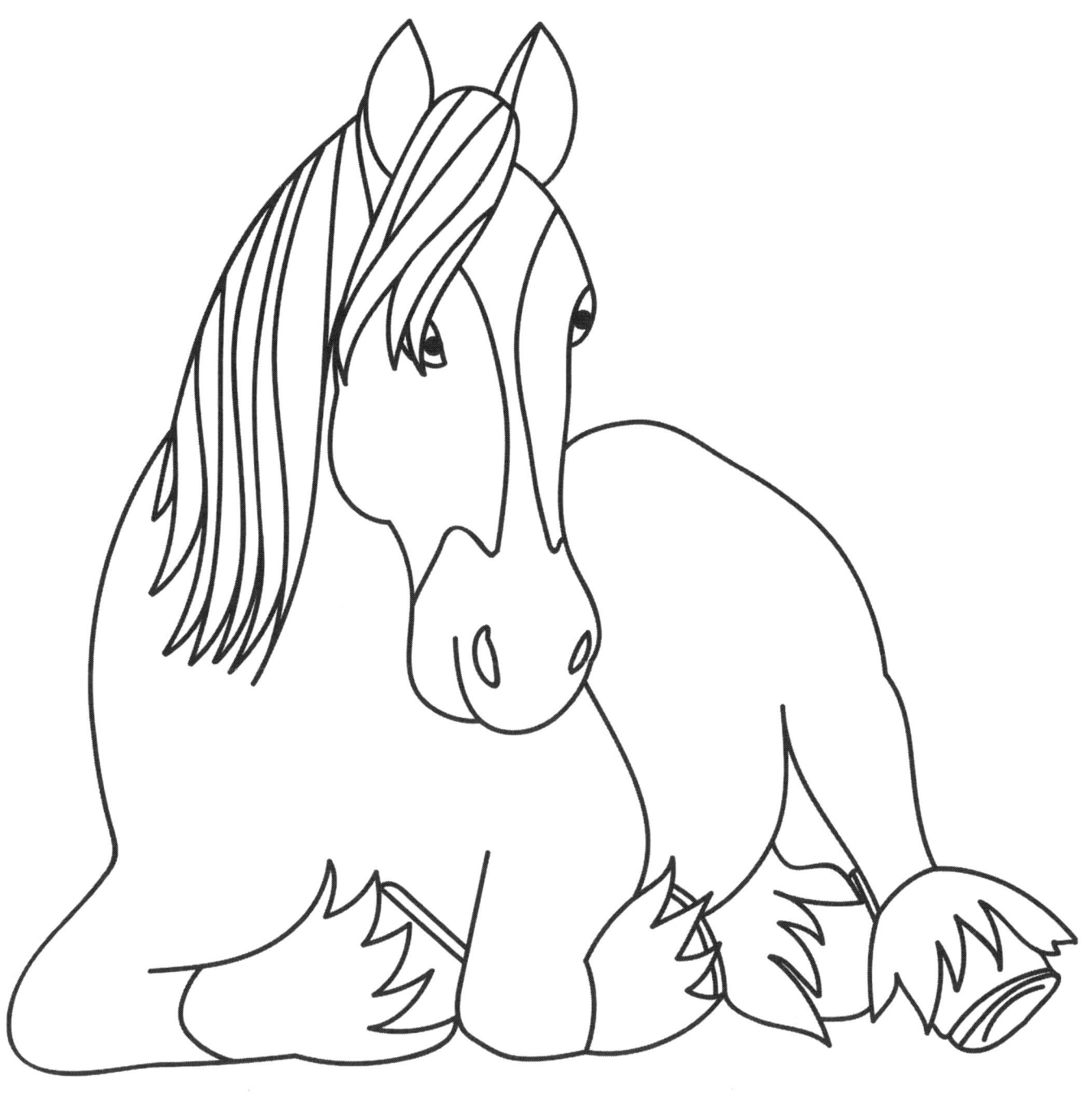

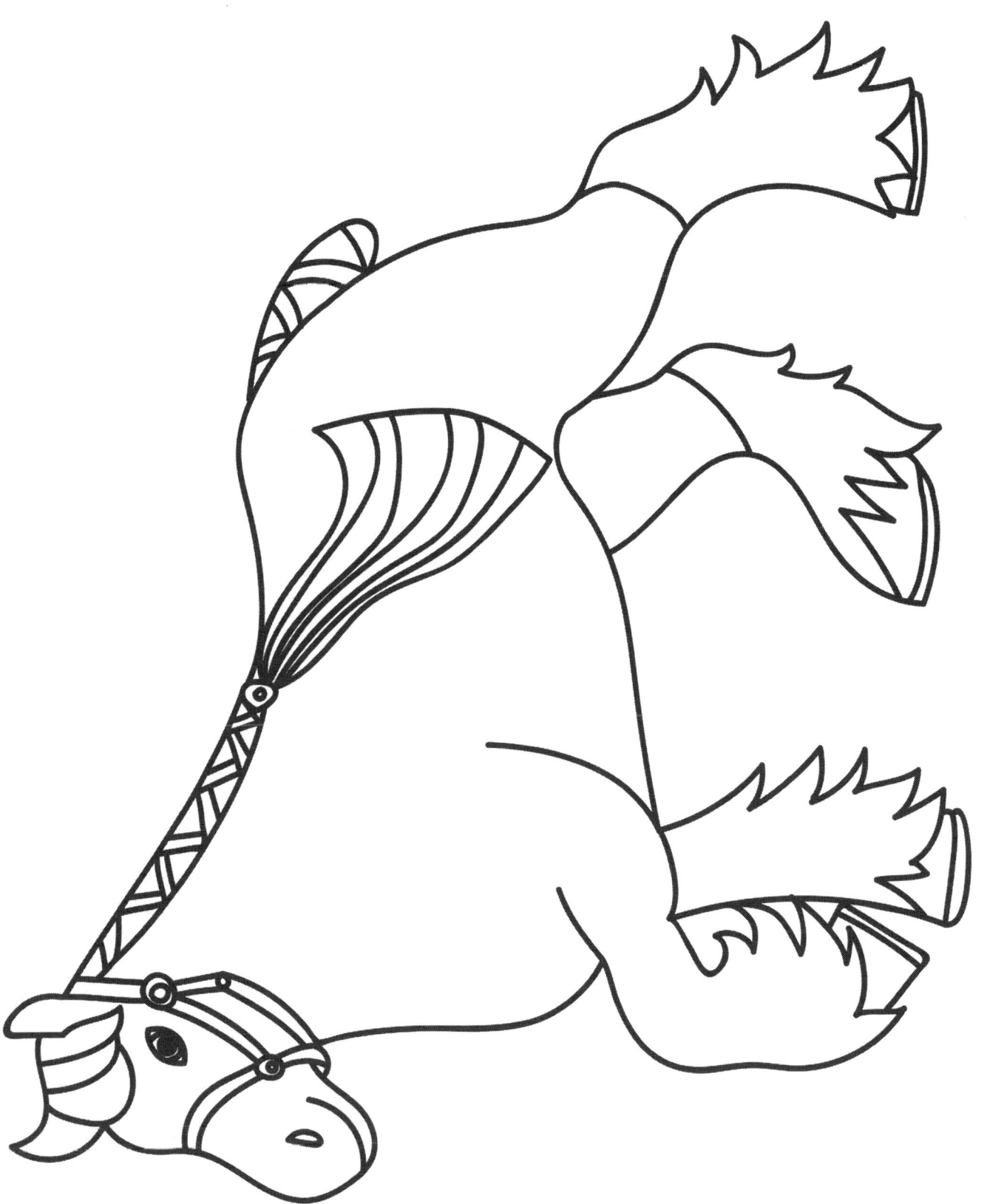

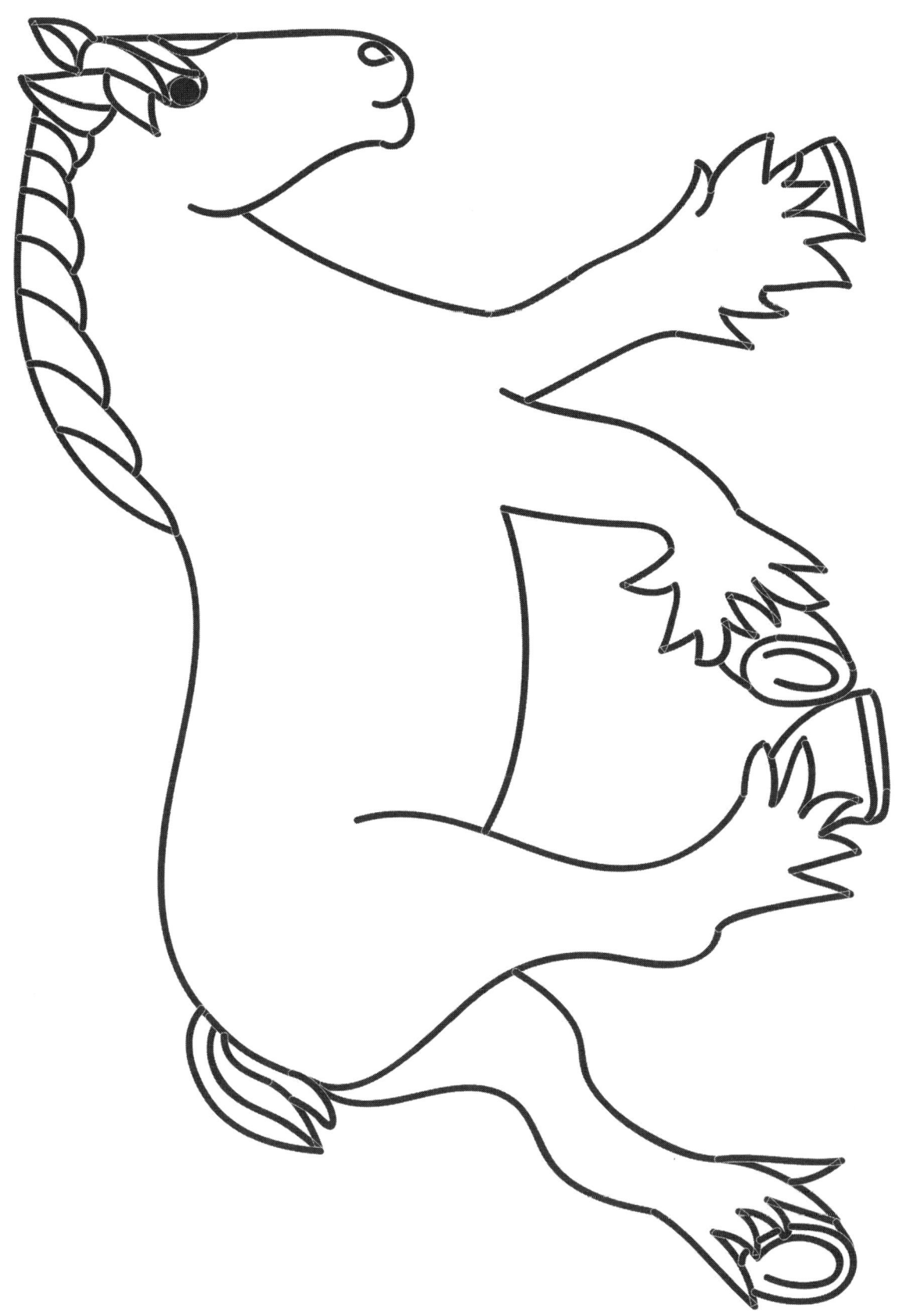

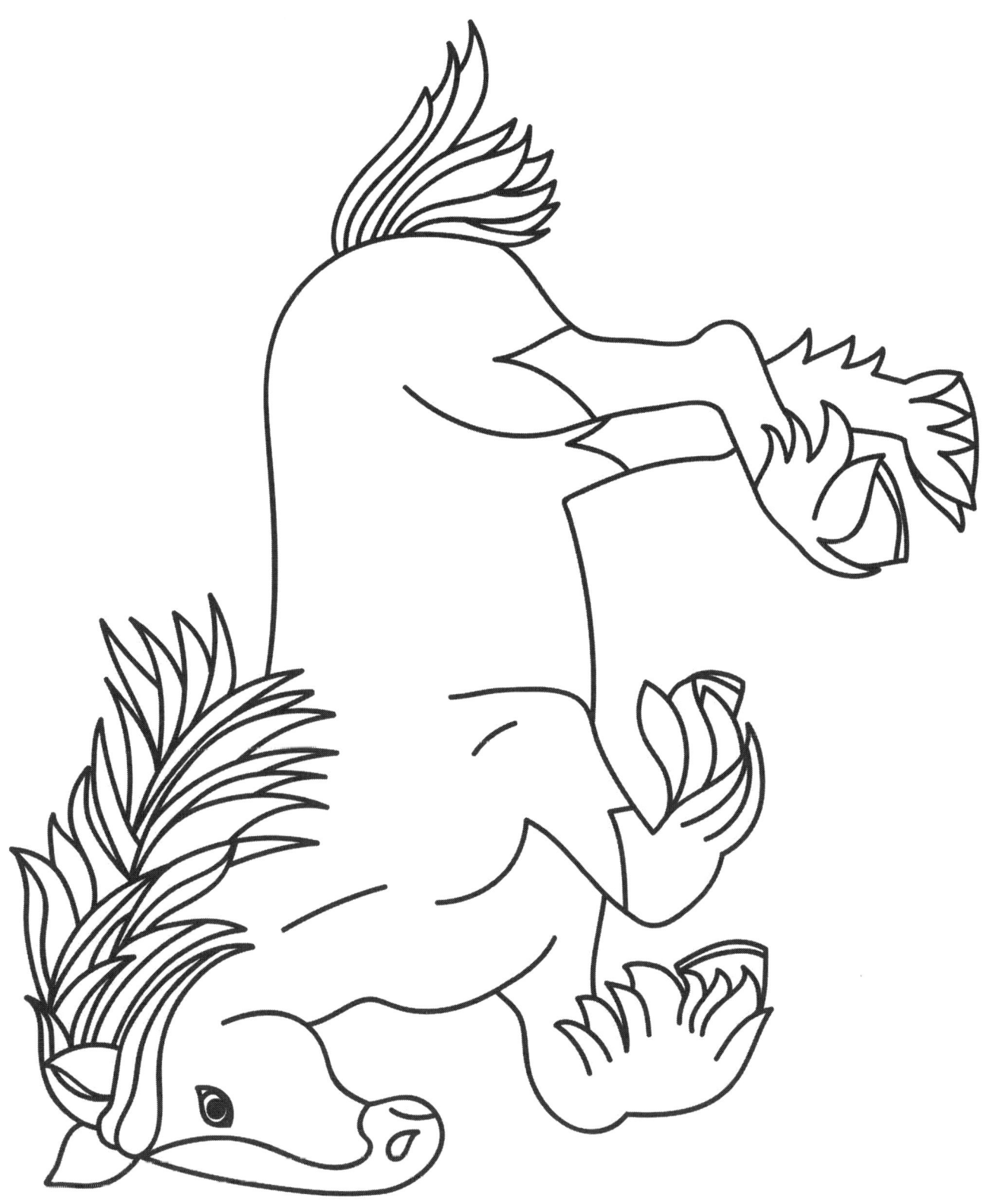

COLOR TEST PAGE

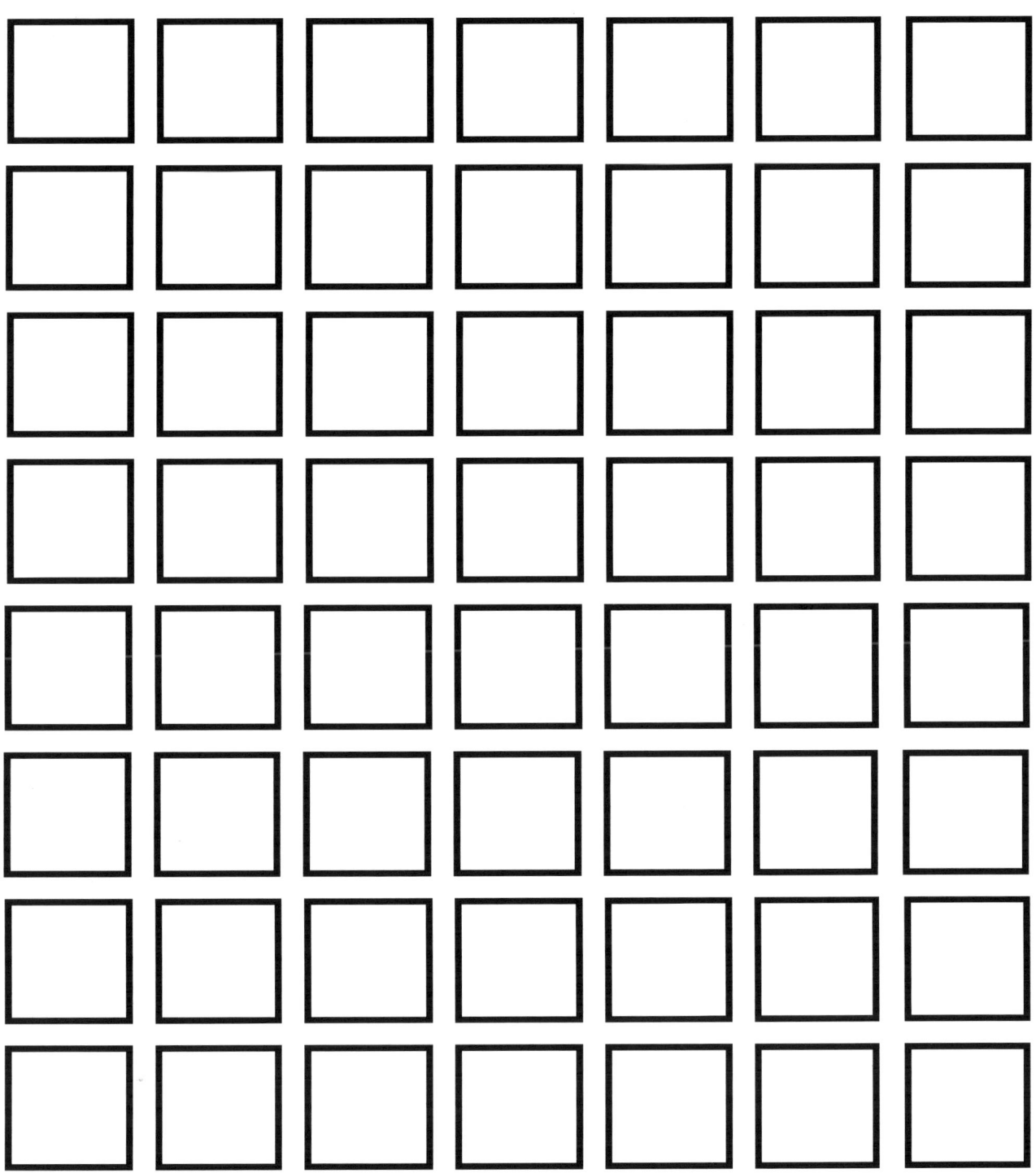

COLOR TEST PAGE

Printed in Great Britain
by Amazon